T0149460

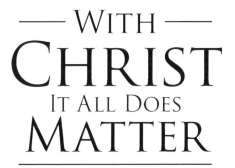

— WITH —
CHRIST
IT ALL DOES
MATTER

BARRY L. LAWTON, M. DIV

WESTBOW
P R E S S®
A DIVISION OF THOMAS NELSON
& ZONDERVAN

WestBow Press books may be ordered through booksellers or by contacting:

WestBow Press
A Division of Thomas Nelson & Zondervan
1663 Liberty Drive
Bloomington, IN 47403
www.westbowpress.com
1 (866) 928-1240

ISBN: 978-1-5127-4780-5 (sc)
ISBN: 978-1-5127-4781-2 (hc)
ISBN: 978-1-5127-4779-9 (e)

Library of Congress Control Number: 2016910527

Print information available on the last page.

WestBow Press rev. date: 7/12/2016

DEDICATION

THIS BOOK IS DEDICATED TO the following individuals.

- To my three sons—Troy, Joshua, and Matthew. Each of them, in their own way, has pushed and challenged me to be the best father and man I can possibly be. I appreciate that.

- In memory of Dr. Kelley Varner, God's prophet and servant. On calling Dr. Varner, he heard the voice of God and took me under his wing. He mentored me in how to study the scriptures, and he spoke directly into my life. Through his teaching, I was able to understand and hear the voice of the Holy Ghost. He imparted God's wisdom, which was in him, into me. How I looked upon the Word of God changed from the very moment I met him. Dr. Varner will always be alive in my heart, mind, and soul. Never will I forget you.

- In memory of Betty Williams, my coworker and friend. Ms. Williams told me that she believed that I would go further, in life once I let go of the "spirit of procrastination." She said that it was controlling me and preventing me from experiencing the greater things God had prepared for me. She said that since this spirit of procrastination has been called out and exposed, it was up to me to seek the Holy

Spirit and be willing to let him remove the evil spirit from my life. I was willing. Thank you. You will be missed.

- In memory of Rev. George Edward Rice Jr. He was/is my best friend. He believed in me when others counted me out. In some of the dark and testing times of my life, he was always there to speak God's encouraging words to continue to move forward. Thank you.

- To my son, Joshua C. Lawton. For many years, he always encouraged and pressed upon me about writing down God's words and sharing them with others. At a very early age, Joshua inspired me to write a book. God used my son to influence and assist me in fulfilling God's work. By faith, this book is a living testimony of my life and God's Word of truth. I will always love you. Always. Your Dad.

- In memory of all my past and present relatives in the ministry of Jesus Christ. Our family has a rich history in bringing forth God's mandate. I recognized that a part of their legacy has been passed down to me.

CONTENTS

Introduction to the Author

WHEN I WAS ASKED TO write this introduction to the author, I knew I had so many things to say about the author that I didn't know where to begin. Our friendship has spanned close to twenty years, and he is an extraordinary man of God with extreme knowledge of the Bible, the Word of God, and life's lessons.

God has blessed him with a gift to hear from God, listen to others, and to speak the truth when counseling others and without putting any individual feelings into it. He seeks the Holy Spirit when it comes to preaching, teaching, and counseling God's people. If you do not want to hear the truth, then do not ask him. He will give it to you straight. And not only straight, but from a biblical standpoint with life applications. Most times when we seek advice (or counseling) from a friend, counselor, or even clergy, we really don't want to hear the truth. Especially when there's a chance of hurting our feelings, thinking to include other people, or when we have to make an important decision about something.

He has told me several times that he had been given the inspiration to write "God's Book" deep inside of him. I am ecstatic that he has finally decided to put what has always been inside him on paper and is willing to share it with others. Men and women of God, I present to some and introduce to others my brother, my best friend, and my confidante, Elder Barry Lawton.

Iris Williams
Tampa, Florida

PEOPLE OF GOD ARE LIVING out a lie based on words spoken by those who have misused or misunderstood the Word of God. By using one's own thoughts, understandings, and opinions, they have compromised God's Word of truth, thereby misinterpreting and misunderstanding the scriptures. This leads the people of God to live their lives according to that person. In other words, becoming someone's "Mini-me." When we receive their compromised words, we end up pretending and acting like we are of Christ. In fact, we are living a life out of the flesh, self, and the influences of this world system. Then there are those who act like they are living out their lives on the worldwide stage. They perform as if they are seeking the Academy Award. Your title, position, status, occupation, or monetary accomplishments do not place you in the kingdom of God. Nor does it place you ahead of anyone else.

The Lord thy God is waiting for that moment when you decide to repent, to seek forgiveness, turn from your wicked ways, and speak only God's Word of truth from your heart. Dr. R. C. Connor states that

> Mental acceptance of truth is not faith. To produce faith, truth must penetrate beyond the conscious mind into the inner center and source of life which is called the heart: our feelings and our emotions. Because truth received intellectually by the mind,

our intellect may be sterile and ineffective; but truth received by faith into the heart, the emotions is always dynamic and life changing.

At the very moment that you receive truth by faith, God sends a spiritual signal of activation from the heavenly realm into your spirit. The Holy Ghost (without) connects unto the Holy Ghost (within), bringing you into the "mind of Christ." In that area of your life, you can no longer play both sides, between God and the world system. No longer in that area of your life, shall you misunderstand God's Word of truth because you seek understanding through the Holy Ghost. You are no longer willing to play church as usual, as you knew it before. No longer are you acting out or deceiving others. Instead, you are walking in the kingdom of God in His truth.

I am so grateful for what has transpired in my life. However, God is not done with me yet. I am thankful to God for all of my experiences that were necessary to bring me to this point of higher ground in my life. The Holy Ghost continues to purge those things not of God out of me. He is my Father, and I am His son, a willing vessel and servant.

Will you receive God's Word of truth and get into a right relationship with God? If you know that God has spoken something into your spirit, seek the Holy Ghost for understanding. There will be mental challenges and struggles to overcome, but you must fulfill what God has placed inside you. For with Christ it all does matter!

About the Cover

AFTER HUMANKIND HAS LISTENED TO the voices of others, tried all that it wanted to do, spoken all of the words it could think of, and reached out for all the things that appealed to its desires, humankind will continue to seek solutions this world system cannot offer. Finally, we come to our senses and remember our "first love"— God. We have journeyed through life's trials, tests, and tribulations. We've experienced life's ups and downs, its small victories and huge disappointments. And now we find ourselves at the edge of what seems like the end of our world. It is here that we find ourselves at the end of the earth (our wit's end) with a large mass of water in front of us. Having experienced those things that are behind us, there is nothing or no one to help us sail to get across the water to something or somewhere else. Looking upward and outward, we begin to focus on the bright and morning star. With our arms and hands raised, we cry out for help and a change of life. A voice speaks from within the bright and morning star and says, "Walk according to My words of truth. Speak only My words of truth, and there you will find the life that you seek."

FOREWORD

J ESUS IS THE AUTHOR AND finisher of this book, channeled by the Holy Spirit through His messenger, Elder Barry L. Lawton.

The true purpose of this teaching is to provide a beam of God's light to all Christians, so they can become beacons of light for the world about God's truths. My favorite scripture in the Bible is, "Trust in the Lord with all thine heart; and lean not unto thine own understanding. In all thy ways acknowledge him, and he shall direct thy paths" (Proverbs 3:5, 6). This book brings forth God's divine intentions that were spoken of Jesus's extraordinary life, to explicate the true meaning behind His messages, and to set the record straight so that we only speak His truth. God only has love for His creations. He does not need to judge us because through Jesus Christ He has forgiven us.

Elder Lawton expressed this collaboration and labor of love became much longer than anticipated. Due to the volume and depth of God's Word and the direction and instructions of the Holy Spirit, he said this book would become the first of a series of three books.

This incredible, mesmerizing, and personal journey is being shown through the eyes of the Holy Spirit in Elder Lawton's life. In this book, your spiritual awareness will be challenged and heightened to experience God's Word like never before. It may even create controversy based on teachings or thoughts that have been passed down from former generations. If you will allow yourself to be open to God's truth, you shall be given an invitation—or gift—toward developing your own personal relationship within God's Word. Then you will be able to access the Christ within you and be forever consciously transformed to whatever level of purpose God has predestined for your life.

It will become your choice whether you believe God's truth or continue to settle for what the world is giving you. I hope you will decide to choose God's truth and receive His knowledge, understanding, ways, and thoughts, leaving behind the crashing waves of frustration, confusion, chaos, unanswered questions, and fear-filled limitations. Walk out of the darkness into the awakening light of God. Walk among the calming ocean waters while navigating toward your destiny.

God values His written and spoken Word so much that He gave us His only begotten Son and His words in a book called the Holy Bible. His written and spoken words are so powerful that He trusted His people would be obedient to Him alone. God's Word—His story—through the Holy Spirit is alive and active. It teaches us how to live life and live it abundantly.

His truth is to transform our lives so that whatever God has you to do, you will do it to His glory. Let your life, your work, your friendships, your goals, and your helping others be a reflection of who God is every moment of the day.

Hazel Bryant
Agape Sabbath Day Church
Brooklyn, New York

PREFACE

THIS BOOK IS A SERIES of inspired words and works from the Lord thy God. I truly believe and know that I received these thoughts and visions from the Lord God and the Holy Spirit. He has led me to write down these words in this book as He presented them. It is not I but He who has given me the inspiration to put this book together. These thoughts and words, I believe, came unto me from Him within my spirit. Out of my obedience to what I believe and know I received through the Spirit of God the collective works that make up this book.

Along the way, I believe and know others were purposely put into place to speak their words of confirmation and guidance. I am so thankful that I had an ear to hear. In fact, this represents some of my life's experiences and testimony.

The day came when I heard my name called. "Yes, Lord," is how I responded. Standing there with me was the Holy Ghost. I was to present my heart before the Lord. Then I heard the voice of the Lord. I promised to speak only His truth as it would be revealed unto me.

For many years I could not explain it. Why was there this uncomfortable feeling in my spirit after hearing some biblical preaching from various ministers and teachers? They were using and speaking from the scripture, but something about what they said, tried to say, or how they said it left me unfulfilled, empty, and/or confused. It seemed that they were leaving out so much of God's Word of truth, skipping over areas of importance and adding more of themselves with their understanding. The Holy Ghost revealed unto me that these additives were called PAPS, and they had nothing to do with the focus of God's Word of truth. What are PAPS? It stands for programs, agendas, plans, and self-centeredness. Now I knew that this was what had been creating deep and troubling concern in my spirit, soul, heart, and mind.

When opportunities did become available, I asked those I thought could provide an answer or explanation to my questions. Instead, the responses I received seemed made up or just another spin added to what I already heard. Sometimes they responded as though I was challenging or threatening their titles, positions, or statuses. In many cases, they avoided me altogether.

As my relationship with God and the Holy Ghost continued to grow even more, I came to a greater understanding of God's Word of truth through the Holy Ghost. I recalled many days when the Holy Ghost guided me and spoke into me about God's Word of truth. And I recalled many nights when God revealed Himself by His Word, depositing and clarifying His ways and thoughts beyond what I could ever possibly think or imagine. My spirit, soul, heart, and mind felt like they were on fire, so I would thirst for more. God continued pouring more and more of His Word of truth and wisdom deep within me. I later found myself drawn to certain individuals who were God's chosen vessels, directly or indirectly. They were there to teach, instruct, proclaim, mentor, and affirm all that God had spoken.

One particular night, the Lord said that I had been chosen to carry a special mantle. I was to go forth and proclaim God's Word of truth. It was important that I learned how to exercise my faith with patience and be not provoked. Then I would have to wait for His given authority and power before speaking His words to His people. I immediately said, "Yes, Lord."

Then something happened to me that has to be explained. I became sick with some type of illness. They called it one thing only because that was the closest diagnosis of the problem. My health went through a series of ups and downs. I ended up getting divorced; I was forced to retire from my job; and many family members and friends were no longer around. It made me wonder if my life was coming to an end. I believed what God had told me and was determined to commit to the Lord even more. As a result of not fainting or giving up, my faith increased. Still, I was puzzled.

Before I could speak the words that had come to my mind, the Holy Ghost stepped in. He told me that I had to be tested, tried, and prepared by God for the journey I was about to embark on. The Holy Ghost wanted—no, the Holy Ghost needed—me to know that this journey was not going to be smooth, easy, or pleasant. He said that I would be hated by many because they don't want God's Word of truth to come forth.

A very dear friend of mine called me one day, and in the midst of our conversation, she stated that a prophetess told her something of a warning for me. How my name came up in their conversation, I did not ask. Anyway, this prophetess had never seen me, and I had never seen her. The prophetess told my friend I would be attacked by a "pack of wild dogs." That was interesting to my friend and me because neither of us had ever heard about wild dogs being in a pack. Not fully understanding what those words meant, I immediately turned to the Holy Ghost for the answer. If this was a message from God, the Holy Ghost would be able to reveal its origin and clarify the message. The Spirit of God spoke directly into me, saying, "Be not afraid."

Be not afraid? That got my attention. Then I remembered a portion of scripture that says, "Be strong and of good courage, fear not, nor be afraid of them for the Lord thy God, he it is that doth go with thee: he will not fail, nor forsake thee" (Deuteronomy 31:6 KJV). My spirit leaped and rejoiced. This was confirmation I needed to get serious about God's plan, to focus on the will of God in writing this (His) book, and to be conscious and prepared as best as possible for what may come my way. Mind you, neither my friend nor this prophetess had any idea what God was doing in my life. Only by the grace of God could something have been revealed, directed, and guided so that I would receive this message. At this point, I told my friend that I knew what the message meant. I told her God had inspired me to write a book revealing certain truths that have been incorrectly spoken. Satan has no power here on earth or in the heavens, but he continues to use our carnal minds and his secret evil agents within each of us to influence our way of thinking. His hope is to use lies and deception to plant doubt and fear in our minds and hearts, to create chaos and confusion among God's people in an attempt to cause people not to activate and engage their faith toward God, and to try and keep us in the shadows of this world system. He will use any means necessary, anybody, or anything to prevent us from relying on God through the Holy Ghost. We must break free and be loosed from Satan's trickery.

The purpose of this book is to provide some biblical understanding regarding God's Word of truths, to provide historical truths that occurred centuries ago, and to provide God's people with a means toward developing a right, personal, and intimate relationship with God through Jesus Christ. By no means is this book an attack on any individual(s), religious beliefs, traditional values, or denominational affiliations. Search the scriptures with the Holy Ghost to learn of God's truth for yourself. The Bible says,

> At that time Jesus answered and said, I thank thee, O Father, Lord of heaven and earth, because thou hast hid these things from the wise and prudent, and hast revealed them unto babes. Even so [This was done], Father: for so it seemed good in thy sight. All things are delivered unto me of my Father: and no man knoweth any man the Father, save [except] the Son, and he to whom so ever the Son will reveal him. Come unto me, all ye that labour and are heavy laden, and I will give you rest. Take my yoke upon you, and learn of me; for I am meek

and lowly in heart: and ye shall find rest unto your souls. For my yoke is easy, and my burden [load] is light. (Matthew 11:25–30 KJV)

In all things, may God's Word of truth stretch your faith. Seek the Holy Ghost for understanding. Let not your heart and mind be hardened to God's Word of truth. Then walk into your newness of life with the Lord Jesus Christ in the kingdom of God.

Acknowledgments

Tʜᴇ ꜰᴏʟʟᴏᴡɪɴɢ ɪɴᴅɪᴠɪᴅᴜᴀʟꜱ ʜᴀᴠᴇ ᴅɪʀᴇᴄᴛʟʏ or indirectly helped guide me in my spiritual growth.

- Apostle Eddie A. Montgomery
- Pastor R. C. Connor, my brother and friend in Jesus Christ
- Pastor P. M. Smith
- Pastor Osborne Robinson
- Pastor Frank M. Reid III
- Pastor Dana Ashton
- Bishop Oscar E. Brown
- Bishop John R. Bryant
- Bishop Clifford Johnson
- Bishop Noel Jones
- Bishop Eddie L. Long
- Bishop Paul S. Morton
- Bishop Walter Scott Thomas
- Bishop Victoré and Pastor Denise Folks
- Pastor Harold Carter Sr.
- Pastor Creflo Dollar Jr.
- Pastor George Dykes
- Pastor Ruby C. Gilliam
- Pastor Bill Hybels
- Pastor G. Emerson Scott
- Pastor Charles Stanley

- Pastor Tim Storey
- Pastor Charles R. Swindoll
- Dr. Samuel Chand
- Dr. Anthony T. Evans
- Dr. Billy Graham
- Dr. Myles Munroe
- Dr. Oral Roberts
- Dr. Melton Short

Disclaimer: This is to make known that the above-named individuals have not officially endorsed this entire book.

INTRODUCTION

WRITING THIS BOOK PRESENTED MANY mental challenges. They were necessary in order to exercise and strengthen my faith. The inspiration of God through the Holy Ghost enabled me to endure many of the obstacles that came my way.

God inspired me to write this book. I asked myself, how? I had never written a book before. Part of me started to feel afraid of what to say, how to say it, and what other people might say about the book. Who was I to write a book? Then God said, "It is not you but I who am writing this book through you. You will receive the words to say." Talk about stretching one's faith.

At the beginning, I went to a few people to inquire about writing a book or who I thought could at least point me in the right direction. None of them gave me the time of day. The one person who has consistently and continuously helped me, press upon me the importance of writing this book, and has helped point me in the right direction to start was my son Joshua. After I got serious about writing this book, God began to send and place me before some of His chosen vessels to assist Him in helping me fulfill His purpose and plan.

According to the Bible, in the beginning God created everything; for everything that was created (or made) was in relationship with everything because everything was in relationship with God. And then something happened! What happened in the heavens came to earth, and it continues even today, in our present lives. It has brought about lies, confusion, chaos, deception, and deceit. You can see this and read about it throughout the scriptures, which is the heart of the matter. The mind-set of Lucifer, who became Satan, continues to influence this world out of our carnal mind. The Bible reads,

> I will ascend into heaven, I will exalt my throne
> above the stars of God; I will sit also upon the
> mount [in the place of control] of the congregation,
> in the sides of the north: I will ascend above the
> heights of the clouds; I will be like the most High.
> (Isaiah 14:13, 14 KJV)

It is Satan who has tempted God's leaders and God's people to establish his kingdom here on earth and to aid in assisting him to ascend into heaven as the father of the people on earth and become like the Most High. What a mind game!

There can only be one King and one kingdom on earth ruled by the Lord Jesus Christ. And there can only be one King and one kingdom in heaven ruled by God. All these other nations, or kings, who are pretending and attempting to build their own kingdoms (or temple, or synagogue, or cathedral, or whatever they want to call it) on earth in place of what God has already established will soon be exposed for what they truly are. Without God and His uncompromised Word of truth, they shall all fall. God holds us to a higher standard of accountability and responsibility because of our commitments to Him. It is His Word of truth, through the Logos (His written and spoken Word), and by His authority and power given unto the Holy Ghost.

A vast majority of God's leaders and His people have either not received or will not accept His uncompromised Word of truth. These people of God would rather have someone feed them a compromised Word of God, or to lean on their own understanding. God's Word of truth is spoken and written. However, many have devised a way to either water it down or mix it with lies (poison)—tainted words of truth and lies—that have been passed down from generation to generation. People of God (just like the Hebrews, who would become Jews, that God brought out of Egypt, who wanted the golden calf) are drawn to an entertaining version of God's Word in order to get excited and to conform to their ways or the ways of another hierarchy of laws and concepts. All the while believing and having others believe in their teachings that it came from God's Word of truth.

In the midst of God's people, there are those who know God and His Word of truth. But the majority of them have decided to remain silent. Instead, they have settled with what has been established by the churches' world system in order to hold on to their titles, positions, statuses, religious beliefs, traditional values, denominational established doctrines, governmental nation orders, imaginations, and the theology of humankind for the purposes of worldly benefits. God's messages and teachings have become mere presentation of one's ability to bring about excitement, entertainment, antics, and loud words with added music. It is as if we have gone to an event that provides what you like: a show, peanuts, popcorn, candy, food, something to drink, and music. Oh, and by the way, there is a cost! Belly full, and you leave with an unfulfilled spirit, soul, heart, and mind craving for something else. Those who remain silent or who continue not to speak of God's uncompromised Word of truth, remember that you are held accountable and responsible for your actions. Jesus said, "Whosoever therefore shall be ashamed of me and of my words in this adulterous and sinful generation; of him also shall the Son of man be ashamed, when he cometh in the glory of his Father with the holy angels" (Mark 8:38 KJV). Could it be that you really like what the benefits of this world system provide you? You pretend to be about winning souls for Christ, but your actions and words show you really do not care one way or the other. Just as long as you obtain and win your goals to get what you want for yourself.

We are to either believe God's Word of truth or throw the

scriptures away. Without God's Word of truth and the Holy Ghost, we will allow Satan's influences to subtly turn us from God to him. No longer can we just engage in, accept, and settle for an entertaining, compromised message of God. We must seek and come to know God's Word of truth. There are those who use Jesus Christ as just a 'product" to obtain worldly benefits for themselves. Your faith, through the power of the Holy Ghost, must be activated and engaged to turn from doubt, fears, lies, and your wicked ways.

Search the scriptures for yourself. Pray unto God, and seek the Holy Ghost for guidance, direction, instruction, and to provide you with the understanding of God's thoughts and ways of His Word of truth. There are those who have been deceiving you. They know you will not study God's Word to prove yourself unto God (2 Timothy 2:15–19). It is God's Word that continues to remind us to "come to repentance" (2 Peter 3:9), to "turn from our wicked ways" (2 Chronicles 7:14), to ask Him to "forgive us our sins" (1 John 1:9), and to "submit yourselves therefore to God" (James 4:7) out of obedience to him (1 Samuel 15:22). Your time has come to begin to get it right and to get in a right relationship with God in all things. For with Christ it all does matter.

CHAPTER 1

IT DOES MATTER

Seek ye the Lord while he may be found, call ye upon him while he is near: let the wicked forsake his money, and the unrighteous man his thoughts: and let him return unto the Lord, and he will have mercy upon him; and to our God for he will abundantly pardon. For my thoughts are not your thoughts, neither are your ways my ways, saith the Lord. For as the heavens are higher than the earth, so are my ways higher than your ways, and my thoughts than your thoughts. For as the rain cometh down, and the snow from heaven, and returneth not thither; but watereth the earth, and maketh it to bring forth and bud, that it may give seed to the sower, and bread to the eater; so shall my word be that goeth out of my mouth: it shall not return unto me void [without fruit], but it shall accomplish that which I please, and it shall prosper in the thing whereto I sent it. (Isaiah 55:6–11 KJV)

IT SEEMS THAT EVERYTHING IN life (including us) matters—except for God's Word of truth. Individually and collectively we are searching for some form of truth that appeals to our pleasure and desires for life. Or we are merely trying to elevate ourselves in materialistic things, position, and status. Unconsciously, we proclaim who we want to be: equal to Christ or God. When questioned about the Word of God, Jesus, and the Holy Ghost, there are some who say, "It does not matter." This could not be further from the truth. All things are based upon the foundation of God's Word of truth. However, this world system continues to build itself upon selfish thoughts and emotional desires in order to achieve worldly benefits. This temporary satisfaction will only last for the moment. God has already torn down these structures and turned all things right-side up that were turned upside down. You see, it does matter.

As Christians, we must search the scriptures with the help of the Holy Ghost to obtain a clearer understanding of God's Word. All truth shall be revealed according to the authority, power, purpose, and plan of God given through His Spirit—the Holy Ghost. The apostle Paul said, "All [Every holy] scripture is given by inspiration of God, and is profitable for doctrine, for reproof, for correction, for instruction in righteousness: that the man of God may be perfect, thoroughly furnished unto all good works" (Ephesians 3:16, 17 KJV).

God's people have been conditioned, controlled, conformed, converted, and compromised into various types of doctrinal beliefs, which are forms of God's Word of truth, in order to fit into some hierarchy of humanity's power. These religious beliefs and denominational doctrines have established their own sets of laws, decrees, and rules by instituting what is called PAPS—programs, agendas, plans, and self-centeredness. Along with their traditional values under certain guidelines, these denominations have created ordinances to promote their particular doctrines.

In addition, I believe there is a great dilemma hindering the spiritual growth of Christians today. Far too often, we have allowed someone else to dictate to us what the scriptures mean without checking it out for ourselves. God does send His chosen vessels to preach and to teach us His Word (Ephesians 4:11). However, we are still held accountable and responsible for knowing it ourselves (2

Timothy 2:15). Why? The apostle John said, "Beloved, believe [trust] not every spirit, but try [prove] the spirits whether they are of God: because many false prophets are gone out into the world" (1 John 4:1 KJV). So how can you try, test, or believe another spirit? Unless you are truly connected to the Spirit of God—the Holy Ghost—you will never know.

Christian education and Bible study are vitally important for your spiritual growth. Yet, in many cases, a Christian education has become no more than a formality or another means of preaching (or lecturing). Besides, an education and Bible study are the least emphasized facets in the body of Christ. Traditional Bible study, for example, can often be very limited in its scope of teaching as it pertains to God's Word of truth. Year after year, what has been presented in biblical teachings are the presumed basic fundamental principles, which are repeatedly spoken to the same group of people. There is very little to no understanding and substance applied to the framework for one's spiritual growth and maturity.

In 2002, the Holy Ghost reminded me of a teaching presented by Dr. Melton Short. He made some very surprising statements about Christian education that have stayed with me throughout the years. With the help of the Holy Ghost, I could relate to what he was saying, and, therefore, I totally agreed with what the Spirit of God revealed unto him. Dr. Short said, "The second saddest fact is that most likely the average churchgoer's grade level in the teaching of the Word of God is probably no greater than the second or third grade." Now, just take a moment to think about that. It is truly sad. How many years have you been in the church? The next statement Dr. Short made was equally disturbing. He said that the saddest fact would have to be that there are so many who do not even know the Lord. This is so true. They may have heard about God, but they don't know Him—even those in the church know about God but don't know Him. And how long have you been in the house of God?

Dr. Melton Short has identified what he believes are the two major problems that must be corrected in our Christian education system as well as within our churches. He said,

> It is widely estimated that more than 90 percent of all Christians live and die without ever gaining anywhere close to what could be a good overall knowledge of the Bible (this means that the church has a 90 percent illiteracy problem), and a small percentage of church's membership ever engages in any systemic, meaningful form of personal ministry that is designed to further evangelize and disciple their family, surrounding neighborhood, workplace, etc. It is almost certain that close to 100 percent of the church's activity is done by no more than 15 percent of its membership. (This means that the church has an 85 percent unemployment problem).

This chapter exposes some of the misrepresented sayings and spoken understandings that do not reflect God's Word of truth. Let not your heart and mind be hardened. Search and study the scriptures. You must pray and ask the Holy Ghost to guide you to understand God's Word. Then you will come to know God's Word of truth according to His purpose for you. For with Christ it all does matter!

The Lord's Prayer

In nearly every church or house of God you have heard these words recited as the Lord's Prayer.

> Our Father which art in heaven, Hallowed be thy name. Thy kingdom come Thy will be done in earth, as it is in heaven. Give us this day our daily bread. And forgive us our debts, as we forgive our debtors. And lead us not into temptation, but deliver us from

evil for thine is the kingdom, and the power, and
the glory, for ever. Amen. (Matthew 6:9b–13 KJV)

But I ask you, is this the truth? Nearly all Christians have come
to accept and believe this to be the truth because of who taught them
and how they were taught from generations past. In fact, however,
it is not the truth.

The truth is this particular portion of scripture is known as the
Disciples' Prayer, which is our prayer as disciples of Jesus Christ.
It is important that we come to understand and know the truth
instead of just believing everything someone says without searching,
checking out, and studying the scriptures for ourselves with the
guidance of the Holy Ghost.

The Disciples' Prayer—our prayer—was given and taught to us
by Jesus. He taught His disciples, and us, how we are to pray to the
Father. False teachings have failed to connect what Jesus said prior
to this, and understanding what He actually said can help clarity
and understanding prevail. Jesus said,

> But when *ye* pray, use not vain repetitions, as the
> heathen do: for they think that they shall be heard
> for their speaking. Be not *ye* therefore like unto
> them: for your Father knoweth what things *ye*
> have need of, before *ye* ask him. After this manner
> therefore pray *ye*… (Matthew 6:7–9a KJV; emphasis
> added)

Could there possibly be another concern or problem in the
church? These false teachings have tried to avoid the truth from
being exposed by the use of vain repetitions of prayer.

The Lord's Prayer is found in the gospel according to John. Read
the entire seventeenth chapter. It is here that you will find the words
of Jesus praying unto His Father, which art in heaven. Jesus prays

for Himself, He prays for His disciples (both for His disciples then and for us now), and He prays for all believers.

It does matter!

MEMBERSHIP

What we say out of our mouths is what has been deposited into our hearts. Where did it come from? It came from what we have chosen to receive, accept, and believe. You need to recognize that within you there are two minds—the mind of Christ and your carnal mind. The apostle Paul tells us,

> For they that are after the flesh do mind the things of the flesh; but they that are after the Spirit the things of the Spirit. For to be carnally minded is death; but to be spiritually minded is life and peace. Because the carnal mind is enmity against God: for it is not subject to the law of God [the Ten Commandments], neither indeed can be. So then they that are in the flesh cannot please God. But ye are not in the flesh, but in the Spirit, if so be that the Spirit is life because of righteousness. But if the Spirit of him that raised up Christ from the dead shall also quicken your mortal bodies by his Spirit that dwelleth in you. (Romans 8:5–11 KJV)

God used Bishop Eddie L. Long to speak the following words: "If you do not understand yourself, in the spirit, you will walk in the flesh, and not in the spirit, but think you're in the spirit." We need to examine ourselves more closely through the Holy Ghost because we are more carnal minded than we choose to believe. Now that is the truth! If we acknowledge it, confess it, repent, and change, we can prevail against it. The Holy Ghost is standing there, waiting on you to decide what you are going to do. Whether you will remain in your carnal mindedness or allow Him to bring you into a newness with Christ Jesus—the mind of Christ.

The Truth: This brings the following questions. Who do you say that you are? Who do you say that you belong to? Whose are you? Who do you say you are a member of? Who is telling you that you are their member, and you belong to them? Whose church do you belong to? And whose roll are you written on? These are very important questions that must be answered. It speaks a lot about you.

Who you say you belong to and whose are you, speaks to your knowing and accepting who you are. This begs to ask, Who told you these things? The apostle Peter said, "But ye are a chosen generation, a royal priesthood, an holy nation, a peculiar people, that ye should shew [proclaim] forth the praises of him who hath called you out of darkness into his marvelous light" (1 Peter 2:9 KJV). Repent, and turn to God, who will tell you who and whose you are and who you belong to.

Who you say you are a member of speaks not only of who you belong to but who is your head (or authority). The apostle Paul says,

> Know ye not that your bodies are the members of Christ? Shall I then take the members of Christ, and make them members of a harlot? God forbid. What? Know ye not that he which is joined to an harlot is one body? For two, saith, he, shall be a man [humankind] doeth is without the body; but he that committeth fornication sinneth against his own body. What? Know ye not that your body is the temple of the Holy Ghost which is in you, which ye have of God, and ye are not your own? For ye are brought with a price: therefore, glorify God in your body, and in your spirit, which are God's. (1 Corinthians 6:15–20 KJV)

Paul is warning us that God forbid us to be a member of a

harlot. The mind of a harlot claims those to belong to them; that's possession. Yes, we are to gather with the other saints toward God in fellowship. However, we must know we are of God. Repent if you must. Whose roll or whose church you claim to be a member of, speaks not only to who you are, who you belong to, and who you say you are a member of. It also speaks to where you will appear when the roll is called. The Bible reads,

> And I [John] beheld when he opened the sixth seal, and, lo, there was a great earthquake, and the sun became black as sackcloth of hair, and the moon became as blood; and the stars of heaven fell unto the earth, even as a fig tree casteth her untimely figs, when she is shaken of a mighty wind. After this I beheld, and, lo, a great multitude, which no man could number, of all nations, and kindreds, and people, and tongues, stood before the throne, and before the Lamb, clothed with robes, and palms in their hands, and cried with a loud voice, saying, Salvation to our God which sitteth upon the throne, and unto the Lamb. (Revelation 6:12, 13; 7:9, 10 KJV)

Is it important, for you to be present and hear your name called at your church? Or is it more important to be present and hear your name called on that day with the Lord?

We should be part of the fellowship with Christ. However, we do not—nor should not—claim that we are members of any church affiliation. Rather, we are members of the body of Christ who fellowship at various houses of Zion. Being a member of some church affiliation is like being a member of some club, group, association, fraternity, business connection, or a clique where you are required to pay dues. We are members of Christ. We are to be committed, accountable, and responsible to God, first, and His leadership for

His glory. Take this moment to repent, to ensure that you remain steadfast to the law of God. Follow the guidance, instruction, and understanding of the Holy Ghost, and, by faith, have hope your name will appear in the Lamb's Book of Life.

It does matter!

CONNECTED TO THE SOURCE

We are perfect. Do you believe that? Jesus said, "Be ye therefore perfect, even as your Father which is in heaven is perfect" (Matthew 5:48 KJV). Could the reason you do not believe that you are perfect is because you do not know who your Father is and who you are? You believe you are in one place (or relationship) with God when, if fact, you are in another place (relationship) with someone other than God. To truly come to know who your Father is and who you are, one must focus on the inner person (spirit) and not the outer person (flesh). Far too many people look at, evaluate, edify, and respect another person based on his or her external characteristics: title, position, status, education, income, possessions, outer appearance, fame, where they fellowship, who they fellowship with, and who they know. This word "perfect" carries with it the meaning of being mature, complete, and fullness. Apostle Paul said, "Whom we preach, warning every man, and teaching every man in all wisdom, that we may present every man perfect in Christ Jesus" (Colossians 1:28 KJV).

The Truth: Stop listening and believing everything other people tell you about who you are or who you are not without the revelation and understanding of the Holy Ghost. The apostle John said, "Beloved, believe [trust] not every spirit, but try [prove] the spirits whether they are of God: because many false prophets are gone out into the world" (1 John 4:1 KJV).

Only God knows the truth about you. No one can speak revelation into your life. If they do, they are unlearned of the spiritual things of God and lack discernment. The Spirit of God shall give someone else the authority to speak and confirm what you may or may not have an unction about. They have come to help give you a boost. It is the Holy Ghost who will reveal what God has placed inside you at the appointed time. Understand that the reason we are perfect in the first place is because the One who resides in us is perfect. It is He who continuously perfects us from the inside-out.

The people of this world system will always judge and condemn you based on what they either think they know or have heard about you (your past). Or maybe they shun you because you do not conform to their ways. The Bible reads, "But the Lord said unto Samuel, look not on his countenance or on the height of his stature, because I have refused [rejected] him: for the Lord seeth not as man seeth; for man looketh on the outward appearance, but the Lord looketh on the heart" (1 Samuel 16:7 KJV).

We are perfect in Christ Jesus, and we are being perfected by the Holy Ghost. It is the will of God that every Christian be conformed to the image of Jesus Christ. To ensure this takes place, God sends His gifts. We find in Ephesians 4:11–16 (KJV),

> And he gave some, apostles; and some, prophets; and some, evangelists; and some, pastors and teachers; for the perfecting of the saints, for the work of the ministry, for the edifying of the body of Christ: till we all come in the unity of the faith, and of the knowledge of the Son of God, unto a perfect man, unto the measure of the stature of the fullness of Christ; that we henceforth be no more children tossed to and fro, and carried about with every wind of doctrine, by the sleight [tricks] of men, and cunning craftiness [cleverness], whereby they lie in wait to deceive; but speaking the truth in love, may grow up in to him in all things, which is the head, even Christ: from whom the whole body fitly joined together and compacted by that which every joint

supplieth, according to the effectual working in the
measure of every part maketh increase of the body
unto the edifying [building up] of itself in love.

The Lord sent His gifts to represent Him for the perfecting of
the saints, for the work of the ministry, and for edifying of the body
of Christ. The Lord actually sent more than just individuals with
gifts to fulfill positions; He empowered His Spirit within them that
is also within you. They are supposed to present the image of Jesus
Christ to others and to speak God's Word of uncompromised truth.
However, humankind, through the world system, has influenced
and tainted what God has sent forward. Many of these individuals
have reverted to controlling, conditioning, conforming, converting,
and compromising God's Word so their beliefs and doctrines can
be enforced. These doctrines either take the place of God or stand
alongside Him. They use PAPS to edify themselves and their religion,
tradition, and denominational platforms. In addition, some speak of,
or edify, their gender while competing, comparing, and complaining
about one to the other's ministry. God's Word of truth has now been
mixed with their lies, tricks, cleverness, and eloquence. They treat
God's people as little children (being ignorant) in order to deceive
them. Know that God sent His Spirit into all His people, not just
a man or a woman. You are urged to pray, ask for forgiveness, seek
His presence, and turn from your wicked ways. Repent, for God is
speaking to all of us. No one is exempt.

It does matter!

WHAT TIME IS IT?

In order to grasp some understanding of time as it equates to
the Bible, one must first recognize that so many changes have taken
place. Changes from what had been originally established by God to
what humanity has rearranged and established in its era as it reflects
today. All of these changes started out based on the solar system and

then changed to the lunar system. It uses the names of gods from various nations, known planets, their languages, individual names of authority, their languages according to who was in authority at that time. There is a significant difference between the established Jewish calendar/time compared to what it is used today.

By having just some of the basic concepts of these calendar/time changes, you may be able to clearly see the differences and the similarities, but you will be able to appreciate and study the scriptures more carefully through biblical history. Even though people have made changes to time and how we understand it, God has never changed! God provided us with a warning that this would happen. He told this to His prophet Daniel in chapter 7, when he received the interpretation of the four beasts. The Bible reads, "These great beasts, which are four, are the four kings, which shall arise out of the earth" (Daniel 7:17 KJV). Later in this chapter, God told him regarding the fourth beast, "And he shall speak great words against the most High, and shall wear out [persecute] the saints of the most High, and think to change times and laws: and they shall be given into his hand until a time and the dividing of time" (Daniel 7:25 KJV).

The Truth: Although other nations had their roles in establishing our time and calendar as we know it today, it was primarily the Roman Empire and the Roman Catholic Church (by the authority of the pope) that executed its power and authority over all the earth. They instituted the changes of the names of the days of the week, the hours of the day, the number of days per month, and the names and order of each month.

Let's compare what the Bible teaches in relationship to what we know today. See illustration 1). God established a seven-day cycle during the time of creation (Genesis 1:1–2:1).

HOURS OF A DAY

Biblical

First watch	6pm (Sunset) to 9pm
Second watch	9pm to 12am (Midnight)
Third watch	12am (Midnight) to 3am
Fourth watch	3am to 6am (Sunrise)
First hour	6am (Sunrise) to 9am
Third hour	9am to 12pm (Noon)
Sixth hour	12pm (Noon) to 3pm
Ninth hour	3pm to 6pm (Sunset)

NOTE:

1. The Jewish day was from sunset to sunset in 8 equal parts.

2. The Roman Empire began its day hourly from midnight to midnight equaling 24 hours.

Illustration # 1

The days of the week were numbered 1 through 7. A numbering system was used all throughout the Bible for everything. It must be noted that God made the seventh day holy; it was known as the Sabbath Day (to be discussed in a later chapter). Today, there is still a seven-day weekly cycle. However, the Roman government and the

Roman Catholic Church decided to give each day a name according to the gods they worshipped. The first day of the week was changed to Sunday. This change was ordered by the pope, so they could worship the sun. It was/is a Roman pagan holiday. The pope ordered the second day to be changed to Monday, so they could worship the moon. The third day was changed by papal order to Tuesday, allowing them to worship the planet Mars, a lesser known Roman god of war. The pope ordered the fourth day to become Wednesday, so people could worship the planet Mercury, another Roman god. The fifth day of the week was changed to Thursday by order of the pope so that they could worship the planet Jupiter, named after Thor, the most important Roman god. The pope changed the sixth day to Friday, which allowed the people to worship the planet Venus, the Roman goddess of love. And the seventh day of the week—the Sabbath Day—was changed to Saturday. The pope ordered it to be done so that they could worship the planet Saturn, another Roman god. We must be very careful in our thoughts about the days of the week. Subconsciously, you might be worshipping the sun, the moon, or planets, were gods of the Roman Empire, without even knowing it.

The hours of a day (see illustration #2) refer to the twenty-four hours that make up a day. The Jewish calendar divided its day into eight equal parts from sunset (6 p.m.) to sunset (6 p.m.). When you do a further study of these eight equal parts, you will discover that each part is broken down into three hourly cycles. Another truth of the matter is that the hour of each day—during that era of time—depended on the length of daylight hours. This meant that it could vary from season to season, day to day, and even in location.

In keeping with the fundamental basics, if we look closer, I believe it also relates to God's creation of time. From sunset to sunrise was called their time of "watch." The time of watch referred to night or evening. It is a time to sleep, to attend to one's family and livestock needs. All for the purpose of restoration and to keep guard. From sunrise to sunset was called their time of "hour." This word "hour" refers to the light of day. It is this time that preparations, work, and fellowship occur. The Bible reads,

> And God said, Let there be light: and there was light. And God saw the light that was good: and God divided the light from the darkness. And God called the light Day, and the darkness he called Night. And the evening and the morning were the first day. (Genesis 1:3–5 KJV)

God uses this phrase, "evening and the morning," six times during creation as reference to the fullness of a day in time. Other nations used the same time frame until the Roman Empire decided they would keep the twenty-four-hour cycle, but their day would begin from midnight (12 a.m.) to midnight (12 a.m.). In addition, they would divide the day into an equal twenty-four-hour cycle.

DAYS OF THE WEEK

Biblical	Roman
1	Sunday
2	Monday
3	Tuesday
4	Wednesday
5	Thursday
6	Friday
7	Saturday

NOTE: The seventh (7th) biblical day of the week is called the "Sabbath."

Illustration # 2

In the Hebrew/Jewish calendar year (see illustration 3), two types of calendars are used. The civil calendar (humankind's calendar) was used to help keep track of the official calendar regarding their kings, childbirth, and contracts. The sacred calendar (God's calendar) was established to remember their various festivals. In keeping with the twelve-month cycle, they adopted the lunar calendar system of twelve months, which alternated between thirty and twenty-nine days per month. The year was shorter than our current calendar, since theirs only had 354 days. However, what they did to adjust for this shortened lunar cycle system was to add an extra twenty-nine-day month every three years. This lunar calendar, or cycle, was accepted by the Babylonians, Chinese, and the Greeks.

Hebrew/Jewish Calendar

Name	Gregorian Calendar	Sacred Calendar	Civil Calendar	Biblical Feasts	Astrology
Nisan [Abib]	March – April	1st	7th	Passover	Aries
Iyar [Ziv]	April – May	2nd	8th		Taurus
Sivan	May – June	3rd	9th	Pentecost	Gemini
Tammuz	June – July	4th	10th		Cancer
Av or Ab	July – August	5th	11th		Leo
Elul	August – September	6th	12th		Virgo
Tishri [Ethanim]	September – October	7th	1st	Tabernacle	Libra
Cheshvan [Bul]	October – November	8th	2nd		Scorpio
Chislev [kislev]	November – December	9th	3rd		Sagittarius
Tevet [Tebeth]	December – January	10th	4th		Capricorn
Shevat [Shebat]	January – February	11th	5th		Aquarius
Adar	February – March	12th	6th		Pisces

Illustration # 3

The Hebrews established four names for the months in the year prior to captivity. These names were hardly ever mentioned in any of the writings of the books of Moses. The first month of the year was called Abib, which was later changed to Nisan. God established this day as the month of beginnings (Exodus 12:1, 2). God had Moses sanctify this day, this month, and this time as the Passover (Exodus 13:1–4). The second month of the year was called Zif (Ziv), which was later changed to Iyar. The seventh month of the year was called Eitanim, which was later changed to Tishrei (Tishri). It was during this month that King Solomon made known that the house of the Lord was built, the ark of the Covenant was installed, and when God's glory filled the temple (1 Kings 8:1–11; 2 Chronicles 5). The eighth month of the year was called Bul, which was later changed to Cheshan (Heshvan). During this month, the house of the Lord was completely finished in all of its parts, according to the words of God (1 Kings 6:38). All the other months were simply numbered accordingly. They were given Babylonian names during the time of captivity in Babylon. Since the lunar calendar cycle was adopted, it is important to note that the lunar year started in the period known today as March.

These names served as a purpose and reminder of both their exodus from Egypt and their exile in Babylon. The Hebrews (who became Jews) would always be able to focus their remembrance toward their deliverance from Egypt and Babylon by the gracious hand of God. The Bible reads,

> Therefore, behold, the days come saith the Lord, that it shall no more be said, the Lord liveth, that brought up the children of Israel out of the land of Egypt, but, the Lord liveth, that brought up the children of Israel from the land of the north, and from all the lands whither he had driven them: and I will bring them again into their land that I gave unto their father's. (Jeremiah 16:14, 15 KJV)

Years later, keeping with the concept of a twelve-month calendar year and the start of the year beginning in the time of March, the ancient Egyptian government made changes to the lunar calendar. First, they changed it from the lunar cycle to a solar one. Second, they established that each month would have 30 days, which totaled 360 days, beginning on the first day. Then they added an extra five days at the end of each year to align with the solar year. Finally, they changed the names of the months to represent their gods.

The next set of changes occurred during the Roman Empire, which was now governing the authority over all the regions. Julius Caesar ordered changes be made to the calendar. He devised using the same solar system as the ancient Egyptians. However, the days of the month would be thirty and thirty-one days long. He kept the month of February at twenty-eight days, but he introduced an extra day in February every fourth year, in what would be known as the leap year. Julius Caesar decreed that the calendar year would begin in January instead of March. He changed the name of one of the months—July—to honor himself. This calendar became known as the Julian calendar. When Augustus Caesar came into power, he changed the name of a month—August—to honor of himself as well.

Pope Gregory XVIII ordered the Julian calendar be removed. Keeping with the same prior concept, Pope Gregory XVIII established that the last day for using the Julian calendar would be Thursday, October 4, 1582. The next day would be the start of the Gregorian calendar. However, Pope Gregory XVIII instituted the change and start date as Friday, October 15, 1582. That is correct! What happened to those missing days? They no longer existed, thus creating more confusion with time. Over the years, the Gregorian calendar made some other minor changes. Although it took years, it was eventually adopted worldwide.

This brings us back to the beginning of this chapter: "What Time Is It?" We may never really know for sure, but God knows the truth. God knows because He established time even though He does not exist in time.

It does matter!

WHAT'S IN A NAME!

Throughout the Bible, God recognizes His people based on who they are in Him. He has given, and permitted various names, titles, positions, and statuses that represent Him and glorify His ministry. we are to carry out the fulfillment of His plans and purpose on earth. It is written in a portion of Our Prayer (the Disciples Prayer) where Jesus taught the disciples to say, "Thy will be done in earth as it is in heaven" (Psalm 6:10 KJV). This means that God's will in heaven should be reflective of our will on earth.

The Bible reads,

> And we know that all things work together for good to them that love God, to them who are the called according to his purpose. For whom he did foreknow, he also did predestinate to be conformed to the image of his Son, that he might be the firstborn among many brethren. Moreover, whom he did predestinate, them he also called: and whom he called, them he also justified: and whom he justified, them he also glorified. (Romans 8:28–30 KJV)

God foreknew and predestined who and what we are supposed to be in Him. It is God who has ordained in heaven what should be recognized here on earth.

However, the influence of Satan, who has no power other than what we permit, continues to affect our carnal mind when we give unto his ways. There are those who have already decided to "will" their minds away from the truth of God to this world system. This world system has turned things upside down, whereas God has turned it right side up. Even in ministry, humankind has promoted and ordained itself based on their worldly perspectives. They use the same names, titles, positions, and statuses as God to further another hierarchy of power that is not of God. They establish names that are not accepted by God. Even the Roman emperor Constantine promoted himself to be the bishop of the Roman Catholic Church to enact certain religious and traditional values and laws.

The apostle Paul warned us of these things through the Word of God: "For I say, through the grace given unto me, to every man that is among you, not to think of himself more highly than he ought to think; but to think soberly, according as God hath dealt to every man the measure of faith" (Romans 12:3 KJV).

The Truth: There are at least four names, titles, positions, and statuses that should never be used in ministry. First, the Bible reads,

> I am the Lord thy God, which have brought thee out of the land of Egypt, out of the house of bondage. Thou shalt have no other gods before me. (Exodus 20:2, 3 KJV)

No person, kingdom, nation, religious rite, or denomination should attempt to rise above or present itself equal God. He alone is the supreme authority over all. All others are imitating God and the kingdom of heaven. Without the kingdom of God, His Word of truth is of the antichrist. They shall be cast out.

Second, no longer is there a chosen group on earth known as priest. Jesus is the Priest. Upon the death, burial, and resurrection of Jesus Christ, all power and authority were given unto Him in heaven and in the earth (Matthew 28:18). It is Jesus who calls upon us to become His priest according to His power and authority. The veil has been torn, so we can come to God for ourselves as well as for each other. Most Christians are unaware of this, or they have forgotten that they can go before God on their own. Or they prefer for someone else to intercede on their behalf. The only one who will intercede on your behalf to God the Father is Jesus. Still, many act just like the Israelites in Exodus 20:18–21.

Third, there are those who have established themselves, recognize themselves, or have allowed themselves to be called "Father." We have an earthly father whose seed was necessary to aid in the process of birth. But no one should ever be addressed or looked upon as "Father" in the ministry of God. This name, title, position, and status belongs to God alone. No longer are we under the ways of the Old Testament. People attempt to use the words of the Old Testament to justify why it should be used as a sign of respect. The Bible reads,

> Now therefore fear the Lord, and serve him in sincerity and in truth: and put away the gods which your fathers served on the other side of the flood, and in Egypt; and serve ye the Lord. And if it seem evil unto you to serve the Lord, choose you this day whom ye will serve; whether the gods which your fathers served that were on the other side of the flood, or the gods of the Amorites, in whose land ye dwell: but as for me and my house, we will serve the Lord. (Joshua 24:14, 15 KJV)

However, we are no longer subject to the laws of Moses in the Old Testament. Rather, we are to follow God's law and the law of grace in the New Testament. Then Jesus said, "And call no man [or woman] your father upon the earth: for one is your Father, which is in heaven" (Matthew 23:9 KJV). With all that was being asked by the Jews—who Jesus was, and who he was in relationship to God—Jesus comforted His disciples regarding this question (John 14:5–21). The Jews looked upon Abraham as their father (John 8:39). Jesus said unto them, "Ye are of your father the devil, and the lusts [desires] of your father ye will do. He was a murderer from the beginning, and abode [lived] not in the truth; because there is no truth in him. When he speaketh of his own: for he is a liar, and the father of it" (John 8:44 KJV).

And finally, the fourth name. The Bible reads, "He sent

redemption unto his people: he hath commanded his covenant for ever: holy and reverend is his name" (Psalm 111:9 KJV). This is the only place in the Bible where the name of God is mentioned as "Reverend." This is God's name, title, position, and status; it is not to be used by humankind on earth. There are other names, titles, positions, and statuses that we must refrain from using.

Within the spiritual ministry of Christ, we have been provided with and accepted by God. Only those who have been approved by God shall walk with Him in the kingdom of heaven. Your name, title, position, status, or what you think you have done do not provide you with an automatic free pass to enter. Jesus said,

> Not every one that saith unto me, Lord, Lord, shall enter into the kingdom of heaven; but he that doeth the will of my Father which is in heaven. Many will say to me in that day, Lord, Lord, have we not prophesied in thy name? and in thy name have cast out devils? And in thy name done many wonderful works? And then I will profess unto them, I never knew you: depart from me, ye that work iniquity. (Matthew 7:21–23 KJV)

Do you truly have a personal and intimate relationship with God that He recognizes? Have you kept the laws of God? Are you speaking only God's Word of truth? Do you know for sure that your name is written in the Lamb's Book of Life? These questions you must answer for yourself. For with Christ it all does matter!

CHAPTER 2

It's the Law

And on the seventh day God ended his work which he had made, and he rested on the seventh day from all his work which he had made. And God blessed the seventh day, and sanctified it [set it apart]: because that in it he rested from all his work which God created and made.

Genesis 2:2, 3 KJV

FROM THE BEGINNING TO THE end of the scriptures, the Sabbath day (or the seventh day) was/is God's holy day. A day of rest. This has not changed. Out of obedience to God, everyone was to rest from work [labor] or household chores, planting and cultivating the land, and caring for their livestock. God designated the seventh day of the week (the Sabbath day) to be holy unto Him. People have misunderstood and misinterpreted the Sabbath day as being a Jewish day. However, this is far from the truth. Before Jews existed, there was the Sabbath day. As a matter of fact, the entire world had honored the Sabbath day. The Sabbath day was also their time to worship God through the preaching and teaching of God's Word.

When the Hebrews were led out of Egypt, God placed the remembrance of the Sabbath day in His law—the Ten

Commandments (Exodus 20:1–17 KJV). Obedience unto God is an act of faith toward God. We are telling God that He is in control of our lives. God had made a covenant with humankind, and that covenant was out of the Ten Commandments, which included the Sabbath day (Exodus 31:12–17 KJV). God said, "My covenant I will not break, nor alter the word that has gone out of my lips" (Psalm 89:34 KJV).

When Jesus was here on earth, the Bible reads,

> And he [Jesus] said unto them the Sabbath was made for [for the good of] man, and not man for the Sabbath: therefore, the Son of man is Lord also of the Sabbath. (Mark 2:27, 28 KJV)

Jesus made himself the example—our example—in keeping the Sabbath day. In addition, the apostles and the followers of Jesus honored the Sabbath day.

After reading and studying the scriptures, we find many references pertaining to the Sabbath day in the book of Acts. The Bible says,

> But when they [Paul and Barnabas] departed from Perga, they came to Antioch in Pisidia, and went into the synagogue on the Sabbath day, and sat down. And after the reading of the law and the prophets the rulers of the synagogue sent unto them, saying, Ye men and brethren, if ye have any word of exhortation for the people, say on. And when the Jews were gone out of the synagogue, the Gentiles besought [invited] that these words might be preached to them the next Sabbath. Now when the congregation was broken up, many of the Jews and religious proselytes [converts] followed Paul and Barnabas: who, speaking to them persuaded

them to continue in the grace of God. And the next
Sabbath day came almost the whole city together to
hear the word of God. (Acts 13:14, 15, 42–44 KJV)

And so the apostle Paul, during his missionary journeys honored the Sabbath day and taught many regarding the salvation of Jesus Christ.

So why is it, and how did it come to be that for a vast majority of Christians today, the Sabbath day (the seventh day, or Saturday) has been disregarded? And why was the Sabbath day changed to Sunday? Well, let's begin by carefully researching the scriptures. There is no biblical or scriptural reference recorded indicating that the Sabbath day—the Lord God's holy day–was ever changed. Not by Jesus Christ or the apostles.

What you will discover is that according to the doctrines, laws, and writings within the Catholic Church, there were significant changes established by the authorization of Pope Gregory XVIII, when he finalized and instituted the Julian calendar (see chapter 1 and the subtopic, "What Time Is It?"). Once the Julian calendar was established as the law of the land, the original day of the Sabbath was lost. However, Saturday still became recognized as the seventh day of the week. What the pope and the Catholic Church did was abolish the Sabbath day, believing that the Old Testament laws were no longer in affect after the death, burial, and resurrection of Jesus Christ. In the Bible, Jesus said,

Do not think that I came to destroy the Law or the
Prophets. I did not come to destroy but to fulfill.
For assuredly, I say to you, till heaven and earth pass
away, one jot or tittle will by no means pass from
the law till all is fulfilled. (Matthew 5:17, 18 KJV)

The truth is that the laws of Moses became irrelevant, but the law of God remained intact.

Another change that was instituted by the Roman emperor Constantine and the Catholic Church had to do with the day of worship. The Roman Emperor Constantine was a sun worshipper. He acted as if he had converted to Christianity and then made himself a bishop of the Catholic Church. That was when he decided to make Sunday the day of worship, hence "sun" day worship. This became the new day of rest. The new day, as far as he was concerned, was the Sabbath day. Constantine, Eusebus (who was the court bishop of Constantine), and the other bishops declared this would be the Lord's Day. It was officially instituted and established by Pope Sylvester. In the Catholic Church's records it states, "All things whatsoever that it was the duty to do on the Sabbath, we have transferred to the Lord's Day." This very ruling changed/or attempted to change the Sabbath day (God's blessed, sanctified, and holy day) to Sunday. This act of authority of the pope and the Catholic Church was in total contradiction to God.

Thank God, the Jews recognized this truth, and they kept the Sabbath day as God commanded. However, the power of the pope, the Catholic Church, and the Roman regime at that time influenced the vast majority of Christians churches, religions, and other denominations to accept their established order. Still, there is no biblical or scriptural reference of being given the authority by God or His Word to make any changes to His law. This and other changes quickly were adopted and passed down as the law for the land and reestablished from one generation to all the generations that followed. The Bible reads,

> After this I saw in the night visions, and behold a fourth beast [nation or kingdom on earth], dreadful and terrible, and strong exceedingly; and it had great iron teeth: it devoured and brake in pieces, and stamped the residue with the feet of it: and it was diverse [different] from all the beasts that were before it; and it had ten horns [kings]. I considered

the horns, and behold, there came up among them another little horn, before whom there were three of the first horns plucked up by the roots: and behold, in this horn were eyes like the eyes of man, and a mouth speaking great things. Thus he said, The fourth beast shall be the fourth kingdom upon earth, which shall devour the whole earth, and shall tread it down, and break it in pieces. And the ten horns out of this kingdom, are ten kings that shall arise: and another shall arise after them; and he shall be diverse [different] from the first, and he shall subdue three kings. And he shall speak great words against the most High, and think to change times and laws: and they shall be given into his hand until a time and times and the dividing of time. (Daniel 7:7, 8, 23–25 KJV)

The prophet Daniel was given this warning and its interpretation by God.

If these unauthorized, unbiblical changes were made and do not appear as biblical truths, why are they taught, practiced, and protected? In other words, they have broken God's law. We are unlawfully—intentionally or unintentionally—following a mandate established by humankind with no biblical basis. Since God has not provided His authorized approval, we are operating in disobedience of God's law and God's Word of truth. Jesus said,

Every plant, which my heavenly Father hath not planted, shall be rooted up. Let them alone: they be blind leaders of the blind. And if the blind lead the blind, both shall fall into the ditch. (Matthew 15:13, 14)

The Bible tells us to

> Remember the Sabbath day, to keep it holy. Six days shalt thou labour, and do all thy work: but the seventh day is the Sabbath of the Lord thy God: in it thou shalt not do any work, thou, nor thy son, nor thy daughter, thy manservant, nor thy maidservant, nor thy cattle, nor thy stranger that is within thy gates: for in six days the Lord made heaven and earth, the sea, and all that in them is, and rested the seventh day: wherefore the Lord blessed the Sabbath day, and hallowed it. (Exodus 20:8–11 KJV)

The Lord made it very clear and direct that this day—the Sabbath day—is to be made holy. No one can arbitrarily change God's law to fit an agenda. Are we continuing to repeat and follow the same deceptions and disobediences that separated us from God in the beginning? The Bible reads,

> And the Lord God commanded, the man [humankind], saying, Of every tree of the garden thou mayest freely eat: but of the tree of the knowledge of good and evil, thou shalt not eat of it: for in the day that thou eatest thereof thou shalt surely die. (Genesis 2:16, 17 KJV)

So what was the purpose for making these changes? Simply put, if you can get people to question the words and teachings of Jesus Christ, you can begin to promote and establish your religious hierarchy of government either alongside God or above Him. Satan is so subtly attempting to overtake God's people as his own. But by the grace of Jesus Christ, our time has been to "repent," ask the Lord for forgiveness, and then get right with God. The Bible says, "And if it seem evil unto you to serve the Lord, choose you this day whom ye will serve; whether the gods which your fathers served that were on the other side of the flood, or the gods of the Amorites, in whose land ye dwell: but as for me and my house, we will serve the Lord" (Joshua 24:15 KJV).

Finally, we must understand that there is no such day or time as "Sunday worship" as a day set apart for worshipping God. We are able to worship God on Sunday or any other day of the week. It is, and it remains, that the Sabbath is the only day set a part for the Lord thy God. And the Sabbath day is recognized by God as an appropriate time to worship Him. The Bible reads, "God is a spirit: and they that worship him must worship him in spirit and in truth" (John 4:24 KJV). You are not worshipping a day!

Still, because of all that has been established and taken place, the vast majority of Christians have chosen to worship God on Sunday in recognition of the resurrection of Jesus Christ. However, neither Jesus nor the apostles acknowledge that a change took place. They recognized what God had established—the Sabbath day (the seventh day). For with Christ it all does matter!

CHAPTER 3

TWISTED TO FIT

*Every man according as he purposeth in his heart,
so let him give; not grudgingly, or of necessity
[unwillingly]; for God loveth a cheerful giver.*

2 Corinthians 9:7 KJV

THIS PARTICULAR SUBJECT SEEMED TO be off-limits to question
or discuss even though there has been more demand, debate,
and deception as to the validity regarding to tithing. As Christians,
we look to our leaders to teach and to preach to us about the truth of
God's Word. It is important to know the scriptural truth as it pertains
to the principles of tithing and giving. Our leaders emphasize that
the scriptures support their claims about God's mandate to tithe. As
true as this may seem, there are no scriptural (or biblical) references
about tithing one's personal income (money) according to the law of
Moses. Nor is there any scriptural (or biblical) reference to tithing
taught by Jesus or the apostle Paul. However, we are to give whatever
we can out of the heart.

If you have studied the scriptures, did you ever ask, "Show me
in the Bible where it says we are to tithe of our personal financial
income as mandated by God?" Let's take a look at the examples used
for tithing. This will be presented in four parts. Part 1 relates to the

Old Testament; part 2 relates to the New Testament; part 3 covers the history of how tithing was instituted. Part 4 explains why the principle of giving, not tithing, should be implemented. Tithing, in itself, was under the Old Covenant through the law of Moses. Giving is under the New Covenant (the law of grace) through Jesus Christ.

PART 1: THE OLD COVENANT

The word for "tithe" in the Hebrew language is *maasrah* (mah-as-raw), which means "a tenth." It is derived from its root word *awshar*, which means to accumulate or to grow rich. The Greek root word is *dekate*, which means "a tenth."

The first reference of tithing is mentioned regarding Abram (who became Abraham). The Bible reads,

> And Melchizedek king of Salem [which would become Jerusalem later on] brought forth bread and wine; and he was the priest of the most high God. And he blessed him, and said, Blessed be Abram of the most high God, possessor of heaven and earth: and blessed be the most high God, which hath delivered thine enemies into thy hand. And he gave him [Melchizedek] tithes of all. (Genesis 14:18–20 KJV)

It must be understood that the Hebrew meaning of tithe in this portion of scripture means to give. Abram (Abraham) had just returned from war against the kings of Sodom and Gomorrah. After winning the battle, Abram took all of the goods of Sodom and Gomorrah; he took all their foods, Lot (his brother's son) along with his goods, and then they left that region of the land (Genesis 14:10–12). When Abram came unto Melchizedek king of Salem, he gave him the tithe (10 percent) of all the spoils from Sodom and Gomorrah. He did not give him any of his personal possessions.

Abram later returned the goods he had taken from the king of Sodom. He did not want to receive anything that was not of God. If we are to use this as an example of tithing, whatever goods we acquire from our enemies, we are to give a tithe (10 percent) of those goods and not our own. As a matter of fact, when you research the scriptures regarding the tithe of Abram, what you will discover is that was the only time he ever tithed of someone else's wealth and not his own.

A second example of tithing in the Bible is in reference to Jacob. The Bible reads,

> And Jacob vowed a vow, saying, If God will be with me, and will keep me in this way that I go, and will give me bread to eat, and raiment to put on, so that I come again to my father's house in peace; then shall the Lord be my God: and this stone, which I have for a pillar, shall be God's house: and of all that thou shalt give me I will surely give the tenth unto thee. (Genesis 28:20–22 KJV)

This portion of scripture is based solely on a vow from Jacob to God. Jacob's vow was mainly about having a relationship with God, yet he placed a condition toward God in their relationship. If God did certain things for him first, he would give a tithe to God and remain in relationship with Him. Now, one of the relevant questions would be since no man has seen God, to whom did Jacob tithe? Realize that this occurred well before there were any Levitical priests. It is my belief that God directed Jacob to tithe through various sacrificial offerings unto God, or by giving to those who were less fortunate than the families of Jacob. Using this example of tithing, it would mean that tithing is based solely on a conditioned vow, which would be given by God.

A third example of tithing is based on the Levites. The principle of tithing used in this portion of scripture is to proclaim God's mandate. The Bible reads,

> And all the tithe of the land, whether of seed of the land, or of the fruit of the tree, is the Lord's: it is holy unto the Lord. And if a man will at all redeem ought [any] of his tithes, he shall add thereto the fifth part thereof. And concerning the tithe of the herd, or of the flock, even of whatsoever passeth under the rod. The tenth shall be holy unto the Lord. He shall not search whether it be good or bad, neither shall he change it: and if he changed it at all, then both it and the change thereof shall be holy; it shall not be redeemed. (Leviticus 27:30–33 KJV)

The Hebrew meaning for the word "tithe" in this portion of scripture is "to pay." This tithe was taken because of the law, not given. Whereas in the other two examples, the Hebrew word for "tithe" means "to give."

God made it explicitly clear that tithing came directly from the seed of the land, the fruit of the trees, and the herd or flock (livestock). It must be noted that tithing was very different from their sacrificial offerings. Tithing was given unto God once yearly, according to the harvest of the land and the yielding of the newborn livestock. The purpose of tithing was to provide the Levites and the priests with those things commanded by God because they had no inheritance.

A fourth example of tithing is based on the Israelites. The Bible says,

> But the tithes of the children of Israel, which they offer as an offering unto the Lord, I have given to the Levites to inherit: therefore, I have said unto them, Among the children of Israel they shall have

no inheritance [no share in the land]. And the Lord spake unto Moses, saying, Thus speak unto the Levites, and say unto them, When ye take of the Children of Israel the tithes which I have given you from them for your inheritance, then ye shall offer up an heave offering [simple offering] of it for the Lord, even a tenth part of the tithe. And this your heave offering shall be reckoned unto you, as though it were corn [any small grain] of the threshingfloor, and as the fullness of the winepress. Thus ye also shall offer a heave offering unto the Lord of all your tithes, which ye shall give thereof the Lord's heave offering to Aaron the priest. (Numbers 18:24–28 KJV)

The purpose of tithing was to be given unto the Levites and the priests; this was God's command. And they were to provide a heave offering, a tenth of that tenth, to Aaron the priest.

Mosaic law (the law of Moses) in the scripture is very clear regarding tithing.

And now, behold, I have brought the firstfruits of the land, which thou, O Lord, hast given me. And thou shalt set it [offer it as an offering] before the Lord thy God, and worship before the Lord thy God. And thou shall rejoice, in every good thing which the Lord thy God hath given unto thee, and unto thine house, thou, and the Levite, and the stranger that is among you. When thou hast made an end of tithing all the tithes of thine increase the third year, which is the year of tithing, and hast given it unto the Levites, the stranger, the fatherless, and the widow, that they may eat within thy gates, and be filled; then thou shalt say before the Lord thy God, I have brought away the hallowed things out of the Levite, and unto the stranger, to the fatherless, and to the widow, according to all thy commandments which thou hast commanded me: I have not transgress thy commandments, neither have I forgotten them: I have not eaten thereof in my mourning [my own distress], neither have I taken away ought [any] thereof for any unclean [unfit] use, nor given ought [any] thereof for the dead: but I have hearkened to the voice of the Lord my God, and have done according to all that thou hast commanded me. (Deuteronomy 26:10–14 KJV)

What we really should do is pray, read, and study over these scriptures while seeking the Holy Ghost for divine truth and understanding.

The fifth example of tithing refers to the message given by the prophet Malachi.

For I am the Lord, I change not; therefore ye sons of Jacob are not consumed. Even from the days of your fathers ye are gone away from mine ordinances, and have not kept them. Return unto me, and I will return unto you, saith the Lord of hosts. But ye said, Wherein shall we return? Will a man rob God? Yet ye have robbed me. But ye say, Wherein have we robbed thee? In tithes and offerings. Ye are cursed with a curse: for ye have robbed me, even this whole nation. Bring ye all the tithes into the storehouse, that there may be meat in thine house, and prove [test] me now herewith, said the Lord of hosts, if I will not open you the windows of heaven and pour you out [empty out] a blessing, that there shall not be room enough to receive it. And I will rebuke the devourer for your sakes, and he shall not destroy [corrupt] the fruits of the ground; neither shall your vine cast her fruit before the time in the field, saith the Lord of hosts. And all nations shall be a delightsome [delightful], saith the Lord of host. (Malachi 3:6–12 KJV)

When God is not speaking directly, He always chooses a messenger to bring forth His words. The Lord thy God chose the prophet Malachi to speak to the people on His behalf. This message was intended for the corrupt priests and the nation of Israel, which had turned away from God's commandments and ordinances to receive benefits for themselves and practice their wicked ways.

In addition to mandating tithes be given to the Levites and the priests, God also exposed the sins of their corruption and wickedness. The prophet Malachi reminded them that they had robbed God according to His commandments and ordinance given and spoken by Moses—the tithes and offerings. Instead, they were keeping the tithes for themselves or tithed things they did not want. They failed to follow through on what was spoken by God in Numbers 18:24–28; they failed to provide for the Levitical priest, and they failed to provide the heave offering to the storehouse. God told them to bring meat (food), not money, to His house (Deuteronomy 11).

Malachi 3:9 reads, "Ye are cursed with a curse: for ye have robbed me, even this whole nation." When we study that verse carefully, we see the prophet Malachi was telling the Levites, the corrupt priest, and the nation of Israel that they were not providing as God mandated, and they had cursed themselves. This scripture has been so misinterpreted. God did not say they were cursed. Because of their disobedience, they brought a curse upon themselves. They robbed God through their disobedience to what He mandated in Deuteronomy 28.

This particular portion of scripture is commonly used to persuade, influence, manipulate, and justify the principles and purposes of tithing. However, this portion of scripture is totally irrelevant regarding any mandate by God for tithing as presented to Christians. It has been misused and incorrectly taught and preached. It misleads believers into a form of disobedience with God and makes someone feel bad or guilty because he or she did not tithe. Let's get this right, tithing—according to today—is neither biblical nor scriptural.

Part 2: The New Covenant

The Pharisees were still governing themselves under Mosaic law. It is well documented that the Pharisees were very wealthy. However, they completely understood that the law of Moses prohibited them from the tithing of their personal monetary wealth. Not even the Sadducees, the scribes, or the people of Israel tithed of their personal monetary wealth. Mosaic law stated that tithing was only of the land, the fruit of the trees, and their livestock. Jesus even said to them, "Woe unto you, scribes and Pharisees, hypocrites! For ye pay tithe of mint and anise and cumin, and have omitted the weightier matters of the law, judgment, mercy, and faith: these ought ye to have done, and not to leave the other undone. Ye blind guides, which strain at a gnat, and swallow a camel" (Matthew 23:23, 24 KJV). Jesus never commanded or told His disciples to tithe, yet He told the Pharisees to obey their own laws.

Again, there are no biblical or scriptural truths spoken or written that God commands us to tithe of money. Nowhere in the Bible is there uttered one scriptural word or verse that tithing was of one's own monetary income. However, there is something regarding money found in Mosaic law. We find in Deuteronomy,

> Thou shalt truly tithe all the increase [what you sow] of thy seed, that the field bringeth forth year by year. And thou shalt eat before the Lord thy God, in the place which he shall choose to place his name there, the tithe of thy corn, of thy wine, and

of thine oil, and the firstlings of thy herds and of thy flocks; that thou mayest learn to fear the Lord thy God always. And if the way be too long for thee, so that thou art not able to carry it; or if the place be too far from thee, which the Lord thy God shall choose to set his name there, when the Lord thy God hath blessed thee: then shalt thou turn it into [exchange it for] money, and bind up the money in thine hand, and shalt go unto the place which the Lord thy God shall choose: and thou shalt bestow [use] that money for whatsoever thy soul lusteth after, for oxen, or for sheep, or for wine, or for strong drink, or for whatsoever thy soul desireth: and thou shalt eat there before the Lord thy God, and thou shalt rejoice [do this with gladness], thou, and thine household, and the Levite that is within thy gates; thou shalt not forsake him; for he hath no part nor inheritance with thee. (Deuteronomy 14:22–26 KJV)

Jesus did not teach his apostles, disciples, or followers to tithe; nor did they. Jesus came to earth to fulfill what was agreed on in heaven. One of those things was the law of Moses. Jesus would eventually become "all," and do what the law could never do. Jesus would fulfill and take the place of the law of Moses, which would exist no more.

The Bible reads,

And when they were come to Capernaum, they that received tribute money [two days' wages] came to Peter, and said, Doth not your master pay tribute? He said, Yes. And when he was come into the house, Jesus prevented him, saying, What thinkest thou, Simon? of whom do the kings of the earth take custom [levy taxes] or tribute? of their own children, or of strangers? Peter saith unto him, strangers. Jesus saith unto him, Then are the children [citizens] free? Notwithstanding, lest we should offend them, go thou to the sea, and cast an hook, and take up the fish that first cometh up; and when thou hast opened his mouth, thou shalt find a piece of money [four days' wages]: that take, and give unto them for me and thee. (Matthew 17:24–27 KJV)

Apparently Jesus did not believe they should not pay taxes.

Furthermore, in all the writings attributed to the apostle Paul, there is nothing written or spoken by him regarding tithing. In fact, the apostle Paul only mentions that "giving" is a sign of faith and love toward God. He spoke of what someone should give and what someone should not give. The apostle Paul said, "But evil men and seducers [imposters] shall wax [go from bad to] worse and worse deceiving, and being deceived" (2 Timothy 3:13 KJV). Just remember that "giving" is not 'tithing."

There is an English word used to identify those types of people; they are called "charlatans." According to the *Reader's Digest of Oxford: Complete Wordfinder,* a charlatan is a person who falsely claims to have a special knowledge or skill. A charlatan—knowingly or unknowingly—becomes a fake, an imposter, a cheat, a deceiver, a double-dealer, a swindler, someone dishonest, and/or trickster. They are being used by the spirit of the Antichrist to misuse, misquote, and misguide God's people away from God's Word of truth. God, Jesus Christ, the Holy Ghost, the cross, and the resurrection are being used only to promote their ulterior motives and agendas. It will be done so subtly in any area of God's written and spoken Word that it becomes twisted. These misdirections are presented in such a way that they appear to be truthful. It is difficult to realize or recognize without the Holy Ghost.

Most if not all of this has been filtrated in and passed down from one generation to the next. Many of God's people will testify and say, "I did not know." Still, there are those who know but would rather keep the lies going in order to receive worldly benefits. Come to know the truth, repent, and change. Your ministry is in error and leading people into the hands of the Antichrist. What is being spoken is a mixed bag of truths with lies—poison. This is what the apostle Paul meant when he said anyone taking and collecting tithes was acting contrary to God's Word of truth, and they are considered charlatans.

According to Matthew 24, Jesus also spoke of them in this manner. The apostle John said,

> Beloved, believe not every spirit, but try the spirits [not the persons] whether they are of God: because many false prophets are gone out into the world. Hereby know ye the Spirit of God: Every spirit that confesseth not that Jesus Christ is come in the flesh is not of God: and this is that spirit of antichrist, whereof ye have heard that it should come; and even now already is it in the world. (1 John 4:1–3 KJV)

This subject of tithing versus giving is far too large for the purposes of this chapter (or book). I suggest you do your own biblical study. Research the book of Acts, specifically chapters 15 and 21. These two chapters will help you gain a better understanding of God's Word of truth pertaining to tithing and giving.

PART 3: THE HISTORY

How did this misunderstanding of tithing versus giving come about? We have discussed the biblical truths of the Old Covenant under Mosaic law and the biblical truths of the New Covenant under the law of grace. Let's now turn our attention to the history of the first Christian church in Jerusalem and beyond.

The first Christian church in Jerusalem was headed by the apostle

James, with the apostle Peter by his side, as well as the other apostles who were still there. The church experienced many struggles within the church and within the region. Primarily, the people wanted to have the things Jesus talked about, but they wanted to keep their religious traditions according to Mosaic law. So the apostle James and the other apostles compromised the teachings and ways of Jesus Christ in order to keep the traditional laws, Mosaic laws, intact. With this compromise, they established the Judeo-Christian church in Jerusalem.

The apostle Paul, however, was given the authority and power to minister unto the Gentiles. This began a debate about what to do with the Gentile Christians. Since they were not of the Jewish tradition or law, the apostle James made another compromise that would completely separate Jewish Christians (who continued under the law of Moses) from Gentile Christians. This way, the Gentile Christians were not obligated to follow the Mosaic law. In order to make this official, the apostle James wrote a legal document and gave it to the apostle Paul for validation, which he could use whenever needed. This authorization included exemption from tithing. One may ask, "What happened to this legal document?" The only ones who would have any knowledge of this would be those living in the Roman empire at that time.

At some point in history, tithing that was established by God changed from what God commanded to receiving money. It was initially supposed to be used to help with the basic necessities of the preachers, the poor, and the conditions of the church. Later, it got out of hand and was misused for the preacher's salaries and family expenses. Because of this, all tithing was abolished.

Nearly three centuries later, after the death of Jesus Christ, the Catholic Church reinstituted the collection of tithes. By the authority and power of the pope, during that time, the principle and purpose of tithing money became the acceptable way of paying the church for whatever the leaders decided to use the monies for; their decisions were not questioned. The Roman Catholic Church also established the positions of someone to be called priest and father. Just like the Levites, instead of God demanding the tithe, the pope demanded people pay their tithes.

Soon, other religious groups and denominations adopted many of the established rules of the Roman Catholic Church, including tithing. They claimed it was of God, which is not true.

Part 4: Giving

According to Jesus Christ and the apostle Paul, we are to practice the principles of giving. It is giving that has replaced the demands for tithing. We are no longer under the law of the Old (Hebrew) Covenant—the law of Moses. Rather, we are under the New Covenant—the law of grace—that is connected fully to the law of God (the Ten Commandments). According to the Old Covenant, God demanded people pay their tithes according to the command He gave Moses.

Tithing was not only demanded but taken. Its purpose was to expose the children of Israel's sins in determining whether they would be blessed or cursed. Tithing is based on the mind-set demanded upon the person (or people). Giving is not demanded or paid. It is not like belonging to a club, fraternity, or anything requiring you to pay membership dues. Giving is expected by God to come from one's heart. Yes, the giving of one's financial possessions is a form of giving of oneself, but it must be out of one's heart. We must learn to give freely out of our hearts. For the blessings of God comes from our hearts, not of humankind's demand.

One of the problems that exist today is that people just want what they want to get what they want. So they go after what they think and hear that they want. In this world, there are many people who act like they are concerned about the souls of other people when, in fact, they are really concerned about themselves and how much money and time they can get out of you.

I do not apologize for telling the truth! Just listen to what they say and how they speak. There are some people who are concerned about the souls of other people, but they have turned their hearts and minds away from God to reap the benefits of what this world might give them. Then, there are some people who are truly concerned about the souls of others, knowing that when God touches them out of their heart, they will be given God's abundance.

Still, God's people may not really know what they want because they have been conditioned to think and feel a certain way apart from the truth of God. It is the Holy Ghost who speaks to your condition. We must repent, ask for forgiveness, and line up under a personal and intimate relationship with God. Upon searching and purging your heart, you will be blessed by the Lord.

Is there at least one example of anyone tithing of their own personal financial wealth in the Bible according to God's Word of truth? The Mosaic law pertained to tithing of the land, the fruit of the trees, and one's cattle (or livestock). With giving there is no limit or demand. What you decide to give is between you and God alone. Tithing was based on God's command of 10 percent during certain times of the year. Giving is a free expression of what you have the ability to give from your heart. Today, tithing is a sin out of disobedience to God's Word. However, giving is a blessing from God, out of God, as an expression to God in your obedience to God.

The Bible reads,

> For he that is dead is freed from sin. Now, if we be dead with Christ, we believe that we shall also live with him: knowing that Christ being raised from the dead dieth no more; death have no more dominion over him. For in that he died, he died unto [to] sin once: but in that he liveth, he liveth unto God. Likewise reckon ye also yourselves to be dead indeed unto sin, but alive unto God through Jesus Christ our Lord. Let not sin therefore reign [rule] in your mortal body that ye should obey

> it in the lusts [desires] thereof. Neither yield ye your members as instruments of unrighteousness unto sin: but yield yourselves unto God, as those that are alive from the dead, and your members as instruments of righteousness unto God. For sin shall not have dominion [rule] over you: for ye are not under the law [the Mosaic law], but under grace [God's spiritual law]. What then? shall we sin, because we are not under the law, but under grace? God forbid. Know ye not, that to whom ye yield yourselves servants to obey, his servants ye are to whom ye obey; whether of sin unto death, or of obedience unto righteousness? But God be thanked, that ye were the servants of sin, but ye have obeyed from the heart that form of doctrine which was delivered you. Being then made free from sin, ye became servants of righteousness. (Romans 6:7–18 KJV)

Yet this portion of scripture has little to do with money. It is about yourself.

So what is the truth? And what has been twisted to fit the ways of humankind? The Bible speaks about this very important matter. Remember, tithing was reinstituted by the Roman Empire first as a tax. The Bible says,

> And they send unto him [Jesus] certain of the Pharisees and of the Herodians, to catch [find some fault] him in his words. And when they were come, they say unto him, Master, we know that thou art true, and carest [fearest] for no man: for thou regardest not the person of men, but teachest the way of God in truth: Is it lawful [right] to give tribute [money] to Caesar, or not? Shall we give,

or shall we not give? But he [Jesus], knowing their hypocrisy, said unto them, Why tempt [test] ye me? Bring me a penny [one day's wage], that I may see it. And they brought it. And he saith unto them, Whose is this image [face] and superscription? And they said unto him, Caesar's. And Jesus answering said unto them, Render to Caesar the things that are Caesar's, and to God the things that are God's. (Mark 12:13–17 KJV)

Again, tithing has become of the world system (humankind) and not God's Word of truth. The world system would have you to believe it is of God when, in fact, it is the mind-set of the world system, which is of the Antichrist. We are of God's Word of truth, so we are to give. As with the questions that were presented to Jesus, it is the same hypocrisy spoken to us today. The question now really becomes, What do we give? When do we give? Where do we give? Why do we give? Who is to give? And how are we to give? The Bible tells us, "But God hath revealed them unto us by his Spirit: for the Spirit searcheth all things, yea, the deep things of God" (1 Corinthians 2:10 KJV). Jeremiah 17:10 (KJV) reads, "I, the Lord, search the heart, I try the reins, even to give every man according to his ways, and according to the fruit of his doings."

God looks upon one's heart. Just because you are not able to meet the demands of humankind, you should not feel guilty. And just because you tithe, don't boast or be prideful. God searches your heart to determine if what you are doing or giving is of Him. God supplies all our needs, which includes giving. Just pray unto God, and make a commitment to Him about your giving. Then watch what He does out of your obedience to Him. Out of His love given to you, you shall be able to cheerfully give and not be ashamed or embarrassed. Let God help you with the little and then He will teach you about the plenty. Keep your commitment unto God as He so directs. Know where you are and what you can do. Let God do the rest. You can't out give God. The Bibles reads, "Give, and it shall be given unto you; good measure; pressed down, and shaken together, and running over, shall men give into your bosom. For with the same measure that ye mete withal it shall be measured to you again" (Luke 6:38 KJV). In fact, this scripture speaks far more than about life than about money. Hear what the Spirit of God—the Holy Ghost—is saying to you.

Here is something else to think about. Understand the concept of what is being said about the giving of your seed. But this, too, has been misrepresented. From the earthly perspective, even when attempting to apply this principle to tithing, if you look at seed as money, God gives us the seed to plant (to work) it in order to bring forth a harvest. According to the Old Testament (the law of Moses) command, they tithe 10 percent from the harvest that was produced from the seed. They did not give 10 percent of their seed. It was their responsibility to plant the seed to bring forth the manifestation of the harvest. The seed produces your harvest, and your harvest makes for the tithe.

Today, God provides you with the opportunity to receive wages (money) or other gifts and skills. You are held responsible and accountable for giving what you can out of your heart. It is God who gives everything.

From the spiritual perspective, the seed is the Word of God. You are a word out of God—His Rhema word. The place where you are to plant yourself is in the kingdom of God. The harvest that you bring forth is the manifestation of God's purpose in your life. Therefore, give that which has been given unto you back to God, and go forth to evangelize. God has called each of us unto Himself to give what we can out of His love and our love toward Him, freely giving abundantly out of one's own heart in obedience to Him.

What does God want us to give? First, He desires that we completely give ourselves unto Him alone. Second, He desires that we obey His commandments, His Word of truth, and His way of life. Third, He desires that we adhere to the direct instruction, teaching, and purpose of His Spirit—the Holy Ghost.

If it is your will and desire to touch the heart of God, trust Him in all things. The Bible says,

> And Jesus came and spake unto them; saying, All power is given unto me in heaven and in earth. Go ye therefore, and teach all nations, baptizing them in the name of the Father, and of the Son, and of the Holy Ghost: teaching them to observe all things whatsoever I have commanded you: and, lo, I am with you always, even unto the end of the world. (Matthew 28:18–20 KJV)

We are to help lead others toward discovering the light of salvation by speaking God's truth. Jesus said,

> For every one that doeth evil hateth the light, neither cometh to the light lest his deeds should be reproved [examined]. But he that doeth truth cometh to the light, that his deeds may be made manifest that they are wrought [made] in God. (John 3:20, 21 KJV)

Help those less fortunate than yourself, and don't be choosey. Your time has come to repent, to ask God for forgiveness, and then to turn from your wicked ways. Jesus said, "If ye continue in my word, then are ye my disciples indeed; and ye shall know the truth, and the truth shall make you free" (John 8:31, 32 KJV). Let's stop getting it twisted to fit what we want. Instead, get into your rightful place of relationship with God for His purpose and plans in your life. For with Christ it all does matter!

CHAPTER 4

THE BIRTH AND DEATH
OF JESUS THE CHRIST

> For God so loved the world, that he gave his only
> begotten Son, that whosoever believeth in him
> should not perish, but have everlasting life.

> John 3:16 KJV

THE BIRTH OF JESUS

FOR AS LONG AS YOU and I can remember, we have been told
to celebrate the birth of Jesus on December 25—Christmas.
However, the problem is that all these many years, we have been told
a lie, which has been passed down from generation to generation.

The Bible is very clear as to when Jesus was born. We just have
to read, study, and discover the truth. One way to know when Jesus
was born is by studying the conception and birth of John the Baptist.
It will be very relevant to refer to the Jewish calendar previously
discussed.

During the first month of the Jewish calendar year—Nisan—
the priests established and continued their rotational duties in the
temple for one week. The priest Zacharias was scheduled to perform

his priestly duties at the temple during the tenth week of the year. This would have taken place during the month of Sivan.

On completion of his scheduled priestly duties for that week, Zacharias would have returned home. It was during this time, the conception of his son occurs, about the third Sabbath of the month of Sivan (Luke 1:5–25). The average term of a pregnancy was approximately forty weeks. This would very well mean that John the Baptist was born in the month of Nisan. This also would have coincided with the Passover and the Feast of Unleavened Bread—Pentecost. Today, the Jews still set up their customary recognition of a special goblet of wine during the Passover Seder meal in anticipation of the arrival of Elijah, based on the prophecy mentioned in the book of the prophet Malachi. The Bible reads,

> Behold, I will send you Elijah the prophet before the coming of the great and dreadful day of the Lord: and he shall turn the heart of the fathers to the children, and the heart of the children to their father's, lest I come and smite the earth with a curse. (Malachi 4:5, 6 KJV)

Even while Jesus was with his disciples, the Bible speaks, saying,

> And his disciples asked him saying, why then say the scribes that Elias [Elijah] must first come? And Jesus answered and said unto them, Elias truly shall come, and restore all things. But I say unto you, that Elias is come already, and they knew him not, but have done unto him whatsoever they listed [desired]. Likewise, shall also the Son of man suffer of them. Then the disciples understood that he spake unto them of John the Baptist. (Matthew 17:10–13 KJV)

This was also mentioned to Zacharias when the angel of the Lord appeared before him (Luke 1:17).

With this information, we can now further our study and focus of attention on the conception and birth of Jesus. The Bible tells us,

> And after those days his [Zacharias'] wife Elisabeth conceived [was pregnant], and hid herself 5 months, saying, thus hath the Lord dealt with me in the days wherein he looked on me to take away my reproach among men. And in the sixth month, the angel Gabriel was sent from God unto a city of Galilee, named Nazareth, to a virgin espoused [engaged] to a man whose name was Joseph, of the house of David; and the virgin's name was Mary. (Luke 1:24–27 KJV)

Do you understand what has taken place? Elizabeth's sixth month of conception (pregnancy) is about the time of Mary's first month of pregnancy with Jesus. When you read and study further (see Luke 1:56, 57), the Bible speaks to us that Mary goes and stays with Elizabeth for approximately three months.

In order to completely understand and know what has taken place, you must be sure to follow along with the Jewish calendar. Let's briefly recap. Elizabeth's conception of her son, John the Baptist, occurred in Sivan, the third month of the calendar year. Six months later, sometime in the latter part of the ninth month of the year—Kislev or Chislev—the conception of Mary's son, Jesus, is noted. Here's something very interesting to think about. Did you know that the first day of the Jewish festival of Hanukkah, the Festival of Lights and the Feast of Dedication, is celebrated on or around the twenty-fifth day of Kislev? And that the Bible states that Jesus is called the light of the world (John 8:12; 9:5; 12:46)?

The Bible tells us that approximately six months after the birth of John the Baptist during the latter part of the month of Nisan, Jesus is born. Was this also spoken of in the Old Testament? Knowing this to be true, Jesus would have been born about the fifteenth day of the seventh month (Tishrei or Tishri). Look at the number! Seems interesting; God's spiritual number for completion.

It was revealed in the Old Testament (or the Hebrew Bible) that God filled the temple, built by King Solomon, during the seventh month—Tishrei (2 Chronicles). It is also mentioned in the book of Leviticus,

> And the Lord spake unto Moses, saying, speak unto the children of Israel, saying, the fifteenth day of this seventh month shall be the feast of tabernacles for seven days unto the Lord. (Leviticus 23:33, 34 KJV)

In the New Testament, it is made clear. The Bible declares that when Joseph and Mary traveled unto Bethlehem, it was just a few days before the Feast of Tabernacles. Joseph had to be present with the other priests and men to pay their taxes (Luke 2:1–7). It would seem that Jesus's birth and the first day of the Feast of Tabernacles are connected.

One thing for sure, the Bible tells us that Jesus was not born on December 25th. So why have we been deceived into thinking that Jesus's birth was on Christmas for all these years? Well, to properly answer this question, one must ask the following question. By whose authority was this day established as the birth of Jesus? The answer: By the authority of the Roman Emperor Constantine. Years later, it was officially declared by Pope Julius I as the birth of Jesus unto the Roman Catholic Church. This was just one of many changes that were authorized by the pope. Understand, the Roman Empire and the Roman Catholic Church had dominated nearly all of the influences regarding the Christian world. Therefore, it was able to reform other churches' religious beliefs, traditional values, denominational doctrines, and the theology of human thoughts about God, His Word, and Jesus.

December 25th was originally a pagan festival or holiday. It was a time to celebrate the annual return of the sun. When noting the season, the twenty-first of December was the shortest day of the year (due to sunlight), and the twenty-fifth of December signaled that the days were getting longer. Since there had been so many changes made to the calendar, and the official records were never disclosed but were stored by the Roman Catholic Church by the authority of the pope, they established and decreed that Jesus would be recorded as being born on December 25th. In addition, to dismiss the pagan holiday, they called this day "Christmas," a day for "mass" (celebration and the communion supper) for Christ. The Bible speaks what is the truth because God's Word is truth.

The Genealogy Count of Jesus to Christ

In almost every Christian church it has been said at least once that Jesus came down through forty and two generations (forty-two generations). They even make an attempt to quote certain scriptures of the Bible—the book of Matthew—to support their claim. Without truly studying the scripture, they have misread, misquoted, misunderstood, and misinterpreted what the Bible actually says. They are only repeating and teaching the genealogy based on what they have heard past generations say. A continuation of misguided teaching incorrectly spoken. There is so much more from the Old and New Testaments that could be shared regarding the genealogy of Jesus that one could devote an entire chapter to. However, for the sake of this portion of study, we shall only present the truth regarding Jesus's genealogy from the book of Matthew that has been spoken and incorrectly been misrepresented.

When you carefully read Matthew 1:1–17, you will see are the timelines and number of individuals represented. Note this is according to Matthew's account under the law of Moses. The Bible reads, "So all the generations from Abraham to David are fourteen generations; and from David until the carrying away into Babylon are fourteen generations; and from the carrying away into Babylon unto Christ are fourteen generations" (Matthew 1:17 KJV). Is that what you read? The Bible does not lie because God's Word is the truth. Yet it is misunderstood, misquoted, and misrepresented about the genealogy of Jesus.

Reread the scripture, slowly, and allow the Holy Ghost to come into your spirit, heart, mind, and soul to receive God's revelation of His Word of truth. From Abraham to David, there are fourteen generations. From David until the carrying away into Babylon are fourteen generations. From the carrying away into Jesus are thirteen generations, which equals forty-one generations. Wait a minute! Does there seems to be a problem with that count of the generations of Jesus? Always know that the Bible does not lie, but how someone misunderstands the Word of God is the problem. Yes, it has been spoken of, preached, and taught that Jesus came down forty-two generations. Now, look closely at the scripture and read. To begin with, one fails to properly understand God's Word without the Holy Ghost. The forty-second generation is not missing. It is spoken of as something that shall come to pass. The forty-second generation has not been fully birthed, or manifested, yet because it is the body of Christ. All of God's chosen people shall be manifested into one body—the body of Christ, the forty-second generation.

The Death of Jesus

Many words have been spoken about, written about, and portrayed regarding the death of Jesus. What is being presented here are the clear truth and awareness about Jesus's death. The Bible, God's Word of truth, dispels all other presentations.

We shall first begin with an essential understanding from the Old Testament. During the period of Moses and the Israelites, one of the laws of Moses addressed what should be done to someone who committed a sin worthy of death. (Pay attention because you will also discover this principle applied in days not so long ago.) An example of such a sin was blasphemy. The Bible reads,

> And if a man have committed a sin worthy of death, and he be to be put to death, and thou hang him <u>on</u> a tree: his body shall not remain all night upon the tree, but thou shall in any wise bury him that day; (for he that is hanged is accused of God;) that thy land be not defiled, which the Lord thy God giveth thee for an inheritance. (Deuteronomy 21:22, 23 KJV)

This indicates the person was marked with a curse.

Understanding the death of Jesus is to understand why He came to earth on our behalf. Jesus made the ultimate sacrifice to remove our sin and guilt (2 Corinthians 5:21); to take away the wrath of God (Romans 3:25,26); to remove all barriers preventing us from reconciling us with God (Romans 5:10, 11; 2 Corinthians 5:18, 19); to deliver us from the curse of the law (Galatians 3:13, 14), the guilt of sin (Romans 3:24), and the power of sin (1 Peter 1:18, 19); to defeat Satan and death (Hebrews 2:14, 15); and to die in our steadfast (place) (Romans 5:8). The life of Jesus was to teach us the ways of God, keeping the law of God, and ushering in the kingdom of heaven. His death, burial, and resurrection set the standard by which we should live and live more abundantly.

During the time of the New Testament, there were still many obstacles of interference in the way, including the corrupt priest, the Pharisees, the Sadducees, the scribes, and the majority of the Jews who did not believe in who Jesus said he was. They were rather content with their own ways of life under the law of Moses. In fact, the leadership felt it was much easier to maintain their rulerships over the Jewish nation, while at the same time reaping the benefits bestowed upon them by the Roman Empire.

When Jesus healed the impotent man who had been at the pool of Bethesda for thirty-eight years (John 5:1–9), the Jewish leadership wanted to slay Him because He healed on the Sabbath day and what Jesus said about Himself and the Father (John 5:10–18). Later on, the Bible tells us,

> Then said they [the Jews] unto him [Jesus], Who art thou? And Jesus said unto them, Even the same that I said unto from the beginning. I have many things to say and to judge of you: but he that sent me is true [reliable]; and I speak to the world those things which I have heard of him. They understood not that he spake to them of the Father. Then said Jesus unto them, When ye have lifted up [crucified] the Son of man, then shall ye know that I am he, and that I do nothing of myself; but as my Father hath taught me, I speak these things. (John 8:25–28 KJV)

At times, the Jews still confronted and challenged Jesus to determine for themselves whether Jesus was the Christ. Jesus said that even though He told them, they did not believe Him (John 10:24–33). Jesus, on the other hand, did not and would not compromise regarding all things His Father led Him to do.

When Jesus was placed under captivity, He was brought before the high priest and other Jewish leaders. According to the Bible, as He stood before the counsel,

> And the high priest arose, and said unto him [Jesus], Answerest thou nothing? what is it which these witness against thee? But Jesus held his peace. And the high priest answered and said unto him, I adjure thee by the living God, that thou tell us whether thou be the Christ, the Son of God. Jesus saith unto him, Thou hast said: nevertheless I say

unto you, Hereafter shall ye see the Son of man sitting on the right hand of power and coming in the clouds of heaven. Then the high priest rent his clothes, saying, He hath spoken blasphemy; what further need have we of witnesses? behold, now ye have heard his blasphemy. What think ye? They answered and said, He is guilty of death. (Matthew 26:62–66 KJV)

In reference to the leading up to the moment when Jesus is about to be crucified, the Bible reads, "And as they led him away, they laid hold upon Simon, a Cyrenian, coming out of the country, and on him they laid the cross that he might bear it after Jesus" (Luke 23:26 KJV). In another portion of scripture, the Bible reads,

And they that passeth by reviled [taunted] him, wagging their heads, and saying, Thou that destroyest the temple, and buildest it in three days, save thyself. It thou be the Son of God, come down from the cross. Likewise, also, the chief priests mocking him, with the scribes and elders, said, he saved others; himself he cannot save. If he be the King of Israel, let him come down from the cross, and we will believe him. He trusted in God; let him deliver him now, if he will have him: for he said, I am the Son of God. (Matthew 27:40–43 KJV)

For the purpose of this reading, we will focus our attention only to the cross. As you look closer into the scriptures and allow the Holy Ghost to open your understanding to what has been spoken and taken place, you will discover Jesus was crucified but not exactly in the way it has been portrayed. People must look beyond what they think they hear and see. When words are spoken, we see the pictures of those words. Speaking of the "cross," we see the image of a cross, the visualization of the cross as it is acted out. It will be misrepresented if we do not understand.

What we have been taught regarding Jesus being crucified on a cross is not the truth. That's right! Jesus was crucified and nailed to a tree. Let this not shock you or make you close your mind to the truth with disbelief. The Greek word for "cross" is *staruos*. In its translation, it refers to any type of upright wooden stake or post. This upright stake in Jesus's crucifixion was a tree that was already securely grounded. What Jesus carried and then later Simon carried was the wooden crossbar, or beam. This was used so Jesus's arms would be stretched out wide on the wooden crossbar. Large nails were then securely driven through His wrists to secure Him to the crossbar. He was then "lifted up" onto the tree with the crossbar secured to the tree. Finally, His feet were placed together, and a large nail driven through His ankles, thus securing Him to the tree. Standing off from Jesus and looking at Him, it would appear Jesus was crucified upon a cross because of His position.

To help you better understand the truth, the Bible reads,

> Then Peter and the other apostles answered and said, We ought to obey God rather [not] men. The God of our fathers raised up Jesus, whom ye slew and hanged on a tree. Him hath God exalted with his right hand to be a Prince and a Savior, for to give repentance to Israel, and forgiveness of sins. And we are his witnesses of these things; and so is also the Holy Ghost, whom God hath given to them that obey him. (Acts 5:29–32 KJV)

Acts 10:39 reads, "And we are witnesses of all things which he did both in the land of the Jews, and in Jerusalem; whom they slew and hanged on a tree."

Acts 13:29 tells us, "And when they had fulfilled all that was written of him, they took him down from the tree, and laid him in a sepulchre."

Galatians 3:13, 14 says, "Christ hath redeemed us from the curse of the law; being made a curse for us: for it is written, Cursed is everyone that hangeth on a tree: that the blessing of Abraham might come on the Gentiles through Jesus Christ; that we might receive the promise of the Spirit through faith."

According to 1 Peter 2:24, "Who his own self bare our sins in his body on the tree, that we, being dead to sins, should live unto righteousness: by whose stripes [wounds] ye were healed."

Jesus's body was taken down from the tree on that day. It was placed in a sepulchre because they were still following their customs and traditions according to the law of Moses. There is a significant difference regarding crucifixion, which was simply being hung *on* a tree (or a wooden stake), along with the crossbar, as opposed to being literally hung *from* a tree.

Considering what took place with Jesus, a curse was turned into a blessing that we received through Jesus Christ. The Bible reads,

> "Father, glorify thy name. Then came there a voice from heaven, saying, I have both glorified it, and will glorify it again. The people therefore, that stood by, and heard it, said that it thundered: others said, An angel spake to him. Jesus answered and said, This voice came not because of me, but for your sakes. Now is the judgment of this world; now shall the prince of this world be cast out. And I, if I be lifted up [crucified] from the earth, will draw all men unto me" (John 12:28–32 KJV).

Jesus Christ was crucified on a tree. He died, He was buried, and on the third day, He arose from the grave. He now sits at the right hand of God in heaven. As we reflect on His goodness, know that we are to always give Him thanks and praise for the resurrection of life. Jesus Christ lives!

THE KEYS

It was on the day of the Passover that Jesus died. What has been spoken, preached, and taught by many of those who worship on Sunday is on that Saturday, while He was still in the tomb, Jesus went down into hell to take back the "keys" from Satan. These keys were supposedly taken from Adam at the fall of humankind. This teaching and preaching is a misguided lie. First of all, Satan has never possessed any keys belonging to God. This biblical untruth was formed out of human imagination. You must search, study, and obtain spiritual understanding and truth by way of the Holy Ghost.

God's keys are also called, the "keys of the kingdom." They are God's authority and power in His decisions that apply to all things on earth. No way would God have allowed Satan to have any hold, possession, authority, or power over the things of this world.

When humankind fell out of direct relationship with God, the keys (or the keys of the kingdom) were returned into the hands of God. The influence of Satan caused humankind to fall out of relationship with God through deception and disobedience to God's command (Genesis 2:16, 17). But if the keys were returned to God, how did they get there? The answer is by the person who had them in the first place while here on earth—the Holy Ghost. The Bible reads, "And the Lord God formed man of the dust of the ground, and breathed into his nostrils the bread of life: and man became a living soul" (Genesis 2:7 KJV). God had given them to His Spirit, the Holy Spirit (or Holy Ghost), so it would have His authority and power to do His will on earth. So when humankind fell out of relationship with God, the Holy Ghost returned, as well, with the keys.

The Bible says,

> For God so loved the world, that he gave his only begotten Son, that whosoever believeth in him should not perish, but have everlasting life. For God sent not his Son into the world to condemn

[destroy] the world; but that the world through him
might be saved. (John 3:16, 17 KJV)

Jesus is the only begotten Son of God and the Word of God (John
1:14). He also came to possess the keys while here on earth.

When did this happened? After being baptized by John the
Baptist, Jesus was led into the wilderness by the Spirit of God (the
Holy Ghost) to be tempted by the devil (Matthew 3:13–4:11). There
He received the keys of God. Shortly, thereafter, Jesus was scheduled
to preach His first public sermon. The Bible tells us,

> Now after that John was put in prison, Jesus came
> into Galilee, preaching the gospel of the kingdom
> of God, and saying, The time is fulfilled, and the
> kingdom of God is at hand [near]: repent ye, and
> believe the gospel. (Mark 1:14, 15 KJV)

The misrepresentation of preaching and teaching about the keys
of the kingdom of God derives from one of two portions of scripture.
First, Jesus said,

> And I say also unto thee, that thou art Peter, and
> upon this rock [this statement, or foundation] I
> will build [establish] my church; and the gates of
> hell shall not prevail [overcome] against it. And I
> [Jesus] will give unto thee the keys of heaven: and
> whatsoever thou shalt bind on earth shall be bound
> in heaven: and whatsoever thou shalt loose on the
> earth shall be loosed in heaven. (Matthew 16:18,
> 19 KJV)

Taking a closer look at this biblical truth, we find verse 18 is
connected with the verses just prior to this one. The Bible reads,

> He [Jesus] saith unto them, But whom say ye that I am? And Simon Peter answered and said, Thou art the Christ, the Son of the living God. And Jesus answered and said unto him, Blessed art thou, Simon Barjona: for flesh and blood hath not revealed it unto thee, but my Father which is in heaven. (Matthew 16:15–17 KJV)

Jesus recognized that Peter received revelation knowledge from His Father in heaven. So based on that statement, Jesus made it known that His church (the body of Christ) would come forth, and hell would not have any place over it. Nowhere in verse 19 does it say Jesus gave any of His disciples any keys of authority and power to make binding decisions on earth that God would uphold. God only upholds those decisions that are in response to His Word of truth, and God rejected anything not directly connected to His Word of truth. God only honors His Word.

Neither would Jesus permit His disciples to be held down or controlled by any religious laws. Only God's Word of truth was to become permanently established in their hearts, minds, and souls. Jesus did not allow His followers to have any rulership over them as long as He was on the earth. Jesus said,

> Think not that I am come to destroy the law, or the prophets: I am not come to destroy, but to fulfill. For verily I say unto you. Till heaven and earth pass, one jot [iota] or one tittle [accent mark] shall in no wise [way] pass from the law [God's Law], till all be fulfilled. Whosoever therefore shall break one of these least commandments, and shall teach men so, he shall be called the least [undesirable] in the kingdom of heaven: but whosoever shall do and teach them, the same shall be call great in the kingdom of heaven. (Matthew 5:17–19 KJV)

What Jesus is saying is that any fellowship of religion, tradition, church affiliation, or denomination that makes decisions outside God's law and God's Word of truth is committing a sin against the will of God. Yet, it was Jesus who gave them power. The power to release others from these religions and traditions were not of God (Mark 7:1–13).

When Jesus was being crucified upon the tree, the Bible tells us, "And when Jesus had cried with a loud voice, he said, Father, into thy hands I commend my spirit: and having said thus, he gave up the ghost" (Luke 23:46 KJV). Jesus had given up His spirit from that mortal body. He was no longer subject to time as we may know of it.

The other portion of scripture that is misrepresented regarding the keys of the kingdom is found in Ephesians. The Bible reads,

> Now that he ascended [went up], what is it but that he also descended [went down] first into the lower parts of the earth? He that descended is the same also that ascended up far above all heavens, that he might fill all things. (Ephesians 4:9, 10 KJV)

Now that you know Jesus sent the keys back to God through the Holy Spirit, and that Satan never had possession of any keys, for what reason would Jesus go to hell? It has been preached and taught that Jesus went down into hell. This is a lie straight from hell. When you read the scripture carefully, it states that Jesus descended into the lower parts of the earth. The problem or misunderstanding (misrepresentation) of this portion of scripture is that the lower parts of the earth are not hell! As a matter of fact, the lower parts of the earth is called "hades," which is not hell at all. Hades, in the Greek language and in the Hebrew language is *sheol.* It is that realm of the earth—the lower parts of the earth—that is the temporary holding (residing) place for the dead or the departed souls who are waiting for Jesus Christ's final return to earth. The Bible reads,

> For Christ also hath once suffered for sins, the
> just for the unjust, that he might bring us to God,
> being put to death in the flesh, but quickened by the
> Spirit: by which also he [Jesus] went and preached
> unto the spirits in prison [hades or sheol]. (1 Peter
> 3:18, 19 KJV)

So what was Jesus's purpose for going into the lower parts of the earth? This is what the Holy Ghost shared with me: To reassure those departed souls and confirm unto them that He (Jesus) was alive, that He would be resurrected, and that the time would come when He would return for them.

Hell, or the lake of fire, is the final place of eternal punishment for all who will not repent, those who have rejected God and His ways, or who God has already sentenced and condemned to hell. This may include those located in the lower parts of the earth on the day of judgment. Only those whose names appear in the Lamb's Book of Life shall arise with Christ to appear before the presence of the Lord thy God. Where will you appear? Or does it even matter?

Jesus did not go into hell to retrieve any keys from Satan. People make it a mystery or want to come to their own understandings or conclusions as to what Jesus did on that Sabbath day (Saturday). Well, I am here to tell you what Jesus did on that Sabbath day. Jesus continued to honor the Word and law of God; He rested. He rested until the time and day to be resurrected from the tomb—on Sunday, the first day of the week.

In the book of Acts chapter 2, God released and Jesus sent the Holy Spirit—the Holy Ghost—to dwell with His believers on earth. And guess what the Holy Ghost brought with him? The keys to the kingdom of God. These are the keys for those who serve God, His law (the Ten Commandments), and His Word of truth. Think about this. If the Holy Spirit resides in you, then the keys to the kingdom of God reside inside you. Until you are connected to the Holy Spirit and God, you will never be given the ability to know or use the keys while on earth. We must be committed to be led by the Holy Ghost and share God's uncompromised Word of truth. Then we will be able to truthfully spread the gospel according to Jesus Christ. And the Holy Ghost will be freely able to inspire us with God's Word of truth throughout the earth. Let's stop poisoning the earth and God's people with lies about God's Word.

Knowingly or unknowingly, we have been led about by a tainted Word of God. We have participated and practiced things that are not of God but, rather, of this world system. We have been led to worship pagan gods and to endorsing the worship of idols. The Bible reads,

> For I testify [say] unto every man that heareth the words of the prophecy [message] of this book [the Scriptures], If any man shall add unto these things, God shall add unto him the plagues that are written in this book [the Scriptures]: and if any man shall take away from the words of the book of this prophecy [message], God shall take away his part out of the book of life [from the tree of life], and out of the holy city, and from the things which are written in this book. (Deuteronomy 22:18, 19 KJV)

The Bible further says,

> And when they shall say unto you, Seek unto them that have familiar spirits, and unto wizards that peep [whisper], and that mutter: should not a people seek unto their God? for the living to the dead? To the law and to the testimony: if they speak not according to this word, it is because there is no light in them. And they shall pass through it, hardly bestead and hungry: and it shall come to pass, that when they shall be hungry, they shall fret themselves, and curse their king and their God,

and look upward. And they shall look unto the earth, and behold trouble and darkness, dimness of anguish; and they shall be driven to darkness. (Isaiah 8:19–22 KJV)

This is a way of worshipping the dead through graven images. The Bible reads,

> Thus saith the Lord concerning the prophets that make my people err, that bite [do harm] with their teeth, and cry, Peace; and he that putteth not into their mouths, they even prepare war against him. Therefore night shall be unto you, that ye shall not have a vision; and it shall be dark unto you, that ye shall not divine; and the sun shall be dark over them. Then shall the peers be ashamed, and the diviners confounded: yea, they shall all cover their lips for there is no answer of God. (Micah 3:5–7 KJV)

This is leading people astray and into a world of temptation, as well as pagan worshipping practices and holidays, apart from God's Word of truth.

Repentance and conversion is a must! Far too many of God's people—believers—have been living a lie because we were taught to believe the lie that was represented to us as being the truth. We must seek the truth even if it hurts us. We must seek forgiveness in order to live a life of obedience and faithfulness unto Jesus Christ. And we must turn from our wicked ways to live a life of righteousness. Until God's way becomes our way, the door to eternal salvation will never be opened unto you (Matthew 5:17–19). Yet, when we come to the knowledge and understanding of God's Word of truth, we will be changed and set free. For with Christ it all does matter!

CHAPTER 5

THE ISSUE IS ...

Love not the world, neither the things that are in
the world. If any man love the world, the love of the
Father is not in him. For all that is in the world, the
lust of the flesh, and the lust of the eyes, and the
pride of life, is not of the Father, but is of the world.
And the world passeth away, and the lust thereof:
but he that doeth [practices] the will of God abideth
forever.

1 John 2:15–17 KJV

OUR ISSUE OF LIFE IS the one thing that causes us to be separated
or to walk away from God intentionally or unintentionally.
This world system is a major reason for it all, but is it? We live in
two systems at the same time: the world system and 'God's Word of
truth. The difference between the two systems can be found in the
words "world" and "Word." It is in regards to the letter "l." Whoever
or whatever has control and authority over you, and whoever or
whatever you have chosen to submit and surrender to determines
which system you are following. Far too many try to use both
systems at the same time in an attempt to reap the benefits to fit
their purposes and goals.

Let's briefly look at these two systems. The world system is controlled by Satan, trying to exert his influence over all matters of life. God's Word of truth has the overall control, authority, and power directed only by God. In this world system, Satan's influences have inserted the letter "l" into God's "Word." This letter represents the lies that are being presented to all God's people so that Satan can get your attention, and have you follow him instead of God. These lies have created and caused us to doubt, disbelieve, fear, be confused, bring about chaos, become a distraction, and bring forth deception. Whether you realize it or not, you will, at times, turn away from your first love—God—to the love of the world system and yourself. In addition, when the word 'world' is used it generally refers to 'culture', or 'a generational era of time'.

As Christians, we must come to know that we belong to God. The Bible reads,

> What? Know ye not that your body is the temple of the Holy Ghost which is in you, which ye have of God, and ye are not your own? For ye are brought with a price: therefore glorify God in your body, and in your spirit, which are God's. (1 Corinthians 6: 19, 20 KJV)

We must submit and surrender ourselves completely to God (James 4:7, 8), continue into obedience toward God (1 Samuel 15:22), develop a faith relationship in God (Mark 11: 22–24), and be willing to increase our trust in Him only (Proverbs 3:5, 6). God's Word of truth is God's way of life. When Jesus prayed to the Father (His Father) for us, He said,

> I have given them thy word, and the world hated them, because they are not of the world, even as I am not of the world. I pray not that thou shouldest take them out of the world, but that thou shouldest

> keep them from evil. They are not of the world, even
> as I am not of the world. Sanctify them as through
> thy truth: thy word is truth. As thou hast sent me
> into the world, even so have I also sent them into
> the world. And for their sakes I sanctify myself, that
> they also might be sanctified through the truth.
> (John 17:14–19 KJV)

The vast majority of God's people are unknowingly being led astray by rejecting God's uncompromised Word of truth while receiving worldly words that tickle their ears (flesh). The Bible says,

> Let no man say when he is tempted, I am tempted
> of God: for God cannot be tempted with [by] evil,
> neither tempeth he [does he tempt] any man: but
> every man is tempted, when he is drawn away of
> his own lust, and enticed. Then when lust hath
> conceived, it bringeth forth sin: and sin, when
> it is finished, bringeth forth death. Do not err,
> my beloved brethren. Every good gift and every
> perfect gift is from above, and cometh down from
> the Father of lights, with whom is no variableness,
> neither shadow of turning. Of his own will begat he
> was with the word of truth, that we should be a kind
> of firstfruits of his creatures. (James 1:13–18 KJV)

There are many people acting and pretending like they are of God. What they have been doing is implementing the works of the world system for themselves and affecting the lives of others. In other words, they are imparting what the world system likes to benefit themselves. Who are they? Well, they have become false prophets. The Bible warns,

Beware of false prophets [those who have turned away from Jesus], which come to you in sheep's clothing [perceiving to be innocent], but inwardly they are ravening [hungry] wolves [a pack of wild dogs]. For there shall arise false Christs [antichrists], and false prophets [those who have turned away from Jesus], and shall shew great signs and wonders [preaching and teaching]; insomuch that, if it were possible, they shall deceive the very elect [God's chosen people]. (Matthew 7:15; 24:24 KJV)

God's will is no longer their first and primary focus. They preferred to lean toward the world system in order to reap the benefits of the world. It's a matter not about eternal life but, rather, immediate and temporary gratification. God's Word of truth is of righteousness, love, joy, and peace; the world system is about corruption, hatred, wickedness, and destruction.

As Christians, we are to declare unto the Lord Jesus Christ and all others that we belong only to God. His Word of truth cannot be compromised as it is portrayed by the world system. Even in the church, God's people have compromised God's Word and themselves with PAPS, which is not of God. Much of what is being promoted as a form of God is, in fact, the influence of this world system and Satan.

The Lord thy God holds everyone to a higher standard of commitment, accountability, and responsibility toward Him and each other. We have been given His Spirit—the Holy Ghost—who possesses God's authority and power for our lives. The Holy Ghost will direct, instruct, provide, and protect us in the ways and thoughts of God's Word of truth.

The Lord said,

Cursed be the man that trusteth in man, and maketh flesh his arm and whose heart departeth from the Lord. For he shall be like the heath [a type of dry shrub] in the desert, and shall not see when good cometh; but shall inhabit the parched places in the wilderness in a salt land and not inhabited. Blessed is the man that trusteth in the Lord and whose hope the Lord is. For he shall be as a tree planted by the waters, and that spreadeth out her roots by the river, and shall not see [fear] when heat cometh, but her leaf shall be green; and shall not be careful [worried] in the year of drought neither shall cease from yielding fruit. The heart is deceitful above all things, and desperately wicked: who can know it? I the Lord search the heart, I try the reins [test the emotions], even to give [repay] every man according to his ways, and according to the fruit of his doings. (Jeremiah 17:5–10 KJV)

This is God's way of determining and knowing who and what you have set your mind to. Whether it be the mind of Christ—God— or your carnal mind—the influences from Satan or of yourself, which is an attempt to combine God's Word with Satan's lies. God searches your heart because your heart should be a reflection of His heart. Your heart will truly express who and what you are in relationship with. Understand and know that what you have received and accepted in your mind, if it is not filtered out, will be deposited into your heart. Your heart will then expose the presence of things you truly have begun to believe by what is spoken out of your mouth and by your actions. If you do not change your ways, it shall become planted and rooted in your soul.

Did you know that the heart of God is not impressed with those things that might get you all excited? You will never be able to mature in God or in the image of Jesus Christ with the materialistic and worldly stuff that is not of God's choosing. If you want God's attention, excite yourself by being obedient to the things of God.

The issues of life can be found within the heart. According to the Bible, it is outwardly expressed through one's control, manipulation, jealousy, uncleanness, covenant breaking, instigation of evil things, arrogance, gossip, envy, lust, lying, resentment, drunkenness, violent reactions, disbelief, negativity, and being argumentative. According to the Bible, it is inwardly revealed by way of someone's despitefulness, unmercifulness, heartlessness, disobedience, deceitfulness, covetousness, unrighteousness, selfishness, unforgiving, greed, dishonesty, distrust, disloyalty, and immoral sexuality.

There are other hidden issues, according to the Bible, that will be exposed: idolatry, ignorance, strife, murder, wickedness, fornication, stubbornness, boastfulness, pride, uncertainty, witchcraft, and flip-flopping of opinions and thoughts. Maybe you walk around, wearing your issues as a badge of honor or despair, such as living to survive or just getting by; going through an illness or sickness; looking for sympathy; being unemployed or experiencing the lack of finances; having your own pity party; going through depression or stress; blaming someone else for your faults; being separated or divorced; feelings of loneliness or feeling sorry for yourself; abusing others or being abused by others willfully and knowingly; expressions of anger, bitterness, and criticism toward each other; and lastly, being paranoid, or becoming suicidal.

Every issue or problem that presents itself in your life can be traced back to the heart of the matter. Whether it be of you or of someone else. This world system desires to steal, kill, and destroy your life. Think about it. There are several churches in the same neighborhood that teach and preach different types of religious beliefs, traditional values, and denominational doctrines regarding God. Each proclaim their version to be the uncompromised Word of God's truth. People living in the same neighborhood receive a different kind of message according to the doctrine and PAPS of that house of worship. Which one is right? Which one is true? Does it make a difference? Does it matter? The Bible says,

> There is one body, and one Spirit, even as ye are
> called in one hope of your calling; one Lord, one
> faith, and one baptism, one God and Father of all,
> who is above all, and through all, and in you all.
> (Ephesians 4:4–6 KJV)

Are we speaking with the voice and sound of the One, true, living God? Or are there many voices and sounds of humankind? Truth be told, for the most part, we have moved to the voice and sound of the familiar in the world. Jesus said,

> I told you, and ye believed not: the works that I do
> in my Father's name, they bear witness of me. But
> ye believe not, because ye are not of my sheep, as I
> said unto you. My sheep hear my voice and I know
> them, and they follow me. (John 10:25–27 KJV)

So the question becomes who are you hearing or listening to? Whose sheep are you, or who do you belong to? Is it the voice of God or your chosen god? Jesus said, "Behold, I stand at the door [your heart], and knock: if any man hear my voice and open the door [your heart], I will come in to him, and will sup with him, and he with me" (Revelation 3:20 KJV). Perhaps you do not know Jesus's voice, so you have let a stranger come into your heart. Perhaps you do know the voice of Jesus, but you have decided to ignore Him because you know you are up to no good and don't want to stop. Or perhaps you have decided to simply listen and lend your ear and heart to someone or something else. By now, you should know what the problem or issue of life is. Let me just come right out and say it: the problem—your problem and our problems—the issue of life is Jesus Christ.

Many of the images and expressions of Jesus Christ are being questioned. God's people are being deceived that Jesus is not the Son of God and only a mortal man. That there is no such thing as the Trinity. That there is another way into heaven and unto God other than Jesus Christ. And that Jesus is merely the product used to receive the worldly benefits of power, control, authority, position, title, status, and yes, money, money, money. The spirit of greed has risen to be perceived as good. The name of Jesus and the cross are being sold like merchandise. It is no longer about truly saving another's soul for Jesus Christ. No longer is Jesus Christ relevant in speaking God's Word. The emphasis is on possessing and establishing one's own church—a worldly kingdom—in order to be edified and to determine just how much stuff one can accumulate.

Because of this world system and the influences of Satan, our churches are being destroyed. Instead of focusing on God's Word of truth in order to live life, we are blinded by temporary things that do not matter. These things are what have caused us problems, concerns, and instability in our quality of life. Humankind's theology and doctrine must be rooted out so Jesus, the cross, and God's Word of truth may be fulfilled without compromise.

Jesus said, "I am the way, the truth, and the life: no man cometh unto the Father, but by me" (John 14:6 KJV). We are either going to believe the uncompromised Word of God and who He is, or we might as well close the Bible for good. Without the authority and power of the Holy Ghost from God, we will probably believe just about anything that is placed before us. People of God, we must be on guard. Any mixture of God's Word of truth (the adding of Satan's lies or another's own point of view) is poison. This brings us to this point. There are those who claim there is another way to get to heaven, before God the Father, called purgatory. It is as if there is some back or side door that you can just go through. What is extremely sad about this is that the influence of Satan is so real and subtle that it has infiltrated our churches, our minds, our hearts, and our souls through deception. Let it be known that purgatory is not biblical or scriptural. It is a business.

Mark 5:25–34 speaks of a woman who had an issue of blood for twelve years. This portion of scripture can also be related to men. Recognize that it is water that gives life, but it is the blood that sustains life. This woman with the issue of blood came to know that the only way to sustain life and to be made whole (well) was to get to Jesus. She made a bold decision to get what she needed. She humbled herself, prayed, sought His presence (His face), and turned from her wicked ways. God answered her cry and forgave her of all her sins. He told her where to go, whom to see, and what to do to be healed of her blood issue. She immediately did as she was told, and was made whole out of her obedience and faith to God. Here is what is also interesting. God the Father and the Holy Spirit did not let Jesus know what was about to take place.

When we attack each other, make false accusations against each other, bash another, blame another, condemn another, crucify another, deny another, gossip about another, lie to or about another, steal or cheat from another, ignore or hide from another, be silent toward another, or fail to help another, what we are actually doing has nothing to do with that person. Rather, your issue is not with that person; your issue is with Jesus Christ. When that person is not acting like you or how you want the person to be, you simply set the individual off to the side. It has been said that "God doesn't call the qualified, he qualifies the called." However, you have made yourself to be the authority. Your carnal mind has been influenced by Satan, and it desires to attack and get in God's way by any means necessary.

Jesus said,

> If ye abide in [remain attached to] me, and my words abide [remain attached to] in [affect] you, ye shall ask what ye will, and it shall be done unto you. Herein is my Father glorified [honored], that ye bear much fruit; so shall ye be my disciples. As the Father hath loved me, so have I loved you: continue ye in my love. If ye keep [obey] my commandments, ye shall abide [live] in my love; even as I have kept

my Father's commandments, and abide in [remain attached to his love. (John 15:7–10 KJV)

In John 15:18, 19 (KJV), He said,

> If the world hate you, ye know that it hated me before it hated you. If ye were of the world, the world would love his own: but because ye are not of the world, therefore the world hateth you.

Since Jesus Christ is the issue, know He is also the only solution. Your life depends on your personal and intimate relationship with Jesus Christ. The Bible reads, "Let us hear the conclusion [the end of the matter] of the whole matter: Fear God, and keep his commandments: for this is the whole duty of man" (Ecclesiastes 12:13 KJV). For with Christ it all does matter!

CHAPTER 6

THE PULLING DOWN OF STRONGHOLDS

For though we walk in the flesh, we do not war after the flesh: (for the weapons of our warfare are not carnal, but mighty through God to the pulling down of strongholds;) casting down imaginations, and every high thing that exaleth itself against the knowledge of God, and bringing into captivity every thought to the obedience of Christ; and having in a readiness to revenge [avenge] all disobedience, when your obedience is fulfilled.

2 Corinthians 10:3–6 KJV

GOD'S WORD OF TRUTH RESEMBLES an onion. Each layer that is being revealed unto us is His truth. But before you can see a layer or peel back a layer, you must first believe in your heart that He is God. Over time, as you receive His thoughts and His ways by the authority and power of the Holy Ghost, you develop the mind of Christ. What prevents us from achieving, discovering, receiving, and believing in God's Word of truth without compromise are these six strongholds. adopted religious beliefs, established traditional values, institutionalized denominational doctrines, worldly imaginations, rooted nations of governmental power, and the theology of humankind. These strongholds are the true stumbling blocks that have caused us to walk outside an upright relationship with Christ.

The vast majority of Christians have been led astray (knowingly or unknowingly) by the five senses of one's soul: attitude, desire, emotion, intellect, and will. Or they just refuse to believe. Instead of trusting in God, humankind would rather lean to its own understanding, according to what they want. If you really want to follow and please God, you must forsake what you want and practice what God wants. Dr. Kelley Varner said, "God is delivering His people from following personalities. Jesus is the Focus. Jesus is the Center. He is enthroned and exalted above all."

Pulling down these strongholds will eventually lead you into the fullness of the kingdom of God here on earth. So let's take a closer look at these strongholds so that you may have a better understanding as to how the enemy uses them against us and toward God.

Religious Beliefs. There is only one religion, if this is what you wish to call it. Your belief should be in the Lord Jesus Christ. The Bible states, "But as many as received him, to them gave the power to become the sons of God, even to them that believe on his name" (John 1:12 KJV). It is Jesus in whom we believe, and Jesus is not a religion. We are spiritual beings in the image and likeness of God. Knowing this to be true, why are we trying to be religious when we are spiritual. To be of Jesus Christ is to be of the kingdom of God. To be of the church world system is to be religious. With this in mind, you now understand your frustrations in this world. You are trying to be something that you are not. The Bible reads,

> If any man among you seem to be religious, and
> bridleth [controls] not his tongue, but deceiveth his
> own heart, this man's religion is vain. Pure religion
> and undefiled before God and the Father is this, To
> visit the fatherless and widows in their affliction,

and to keep himself unspotted from the world. (James 1:26, 27 KJV)

The truth is many of us are more worried about ourselves and what we want than about someone else.

Religion makes an attempt to emulate God. It is outside of the realm of God, like being in a prison system separated from society. Religion keeps the Spirit of God from coming out in order to present truth, authority, and the power of God. At the same time, religion keeps you from walking into where God's Word of truth is. The problem, it would seem, is that they have developed a reprobate mind (Romans 1:24–32). But this is not so for Christians. Christians cannot have a reprobate mind. Why? The Bible tells us, "Therefore if any man be in Christ, he is a new creature; old things are passed away; behold, all things are become new" (2 Corinthians 5:17 KJV). The Holy Spirit has been given unto us to help guide, direct, and instruct us in living a life under God. However, Christians would rather—intentionally or unintentionally—refuse to operate according to the authority and power of the Holy Spirit because it would be unpopular, uncomfortable, or make them have to change their ways of life. They would rather lean to their own understanding (Proverbs 3:5) and the ways of this world system. Therefore, they have become what is known as being "double minded." The Bible reads,

> My brethren, count it all joy when ye fall into divers temptations [various trials]; knowing this, that the trying of your faith worketh [develops] patience. But let patience have her perfect [complete] work, that ye may be perfect [mature] and entire [finished], wanting [lacking] nothing. If any of you lack wisdom, let him ask of God, that giveth to all men liberally, and upbraideth not; and it shall be given him. But let him ask in faith, nothing wavering. For he that wavereth is like a wave of the sea driven

with the wind and tossed. For let not that man think that he shall receive any thing of the Lord. A double minded man is unstable in all his ways. Let the brother of low degree [humble circumstance] rejoice in that he is exalted: but the rich, in that he is made low: because as the flower of the grass he shall pass away. (James 1:2–10 KJV)

In other words, those who have submitted and surrendered themselves to God and are obedient to His Word, shall rise above, while those who have received what they think is much shall fall. Those with a reprobate mind do not have the indwelling Holy Spirit, so they live according to the world system and the influences of the Antichrist.

In the beginning, God made us in His likeness and His image (Genesis 1:26, 27), His Spirit. Because of deception and disobedience, sin entered, and we lost our identities and our ways back to being who we are and our relationship with God. God sent His only begotten Son—Jesus—to take away our sins, remove us from the curse of death, reconcile us to the Father, and provide the plan of salvation to be redeemed. Afterward, Jesus sent the Holy Spirit, who dwells inside every believer, to be our guide, director, teacher, instructor, and comforter. And to lead us in the way that we should go toward Jesus. Even though a vast majority of Christians have acknowledged that the only way to the Father is through Jesus Christ, there are still others who seem to believe there is another way. They disregard the Holy Spirit in order to edify themselves and each other. This way, they can continue living their lives according to their own pleasures and reap the benefits of this world system.

Can you be honest with yourself before God? He knows all anyway. Take a moment, and realize that the real reason you are so frustrated, confused, unfulfilled, dissatisfied, and searching for love is because of religion and its connection to this world system that has imprisoned you. In his song entitled, "Losing My Religion," Kirk

Franklin said, "The truth will hurt you. Or the truth will set you free. What will truth do for you?" The Bible says,

> Then said Jesus to those Jews which believed on him, If ye continue in my word, then are ye my disciples indeed. And ye shall know the truth, and the truth shall make you free. (John 8:31, 32 KJV)

Until you break free from the prison of religion, you will never discover and come to the knowledge and understanding of who you are (your true identity) and who God is. You will never receive and know the wisdom of God's Word of truth. You will remain enslaved to this world system that has a hold on you. You will continue to settle for whatever this world system can or will give you, even if you trample upon others or are trampled upon by others. You will become what will be known as a "Christian settler." God has ordained and predestined you to be and do things according to His purpose and plan for your life. Instead, you are simply surviving life, not living the life spoken of by Jesus (John 10:10).

The Word is Jesus (John 1:1, 2, 14), and Jesus is the way, the truth, and the life (John 14:6). Therefore, the Word and the truth are one and the same—Jesus. Anyone or anything else that is being written or spoken about that is not connected to the uncompromised Word of God is false or poison. Being confined in a prison system that has been infiltrated with poison will eventually kill you. Is Jesus your healer? Then seek God's Word of truth. Break free from those chains, come out, and be free in the name of Jesus!

Traditional Values. The Bible reads,

> Wherefore gird up the loins of your mind, be sober, and hope to the end for the grace, that is to be brought unto you at the revelation of Jesus Christ; as obedient children, not fashioning [shaping up

your way of living] yourselves according to the former lusts in your ignorance: but as he which hath called you is holy, so be holy in all manner of conversation [living]: because it [the scripture ways] is written, Be Ye Holy: For I Am Holy. And if ye call on the Father, who without respect of persons judgeth according to every man's work, pass the time of your sojourning [pilgrimage] here in fear: forasmuch as ye know that ye were not redeemed with corruptible things, as silver and gold, from your vain conversation received by tradition from your fathers; but with the precious blood of Christ, as of a lamb without spot: who verily was foreordained before the foundation of the world, but was manifest in these last times for you. Who by him do believe in God, that raised him up from the dead, and gave [brought him into the presence of God] him glory; that your faith and hope might be in God. (1 Peter 1:13–21 KJV)

When was the last time, or maybe the first time, that you felt free in the spirit? When you were able to pray and praise God, and submit yourself to the unction of the Holy Spirit? No music. No one to direct or instruct you as to what to do toward God in the sanctuary. No limitation of time placed on you. Humankind's way had been totally taken out of the picture. And no one was stopping the movement of God or quenching the Spirit of God. Just you and possibly the congregation, submitting yourselves to the authority and power of the Spirit of God.

As Christians, when we enter the house of God, we should be aware that the indwelling Holy Ghost is within us. The problem (or question) becomes, Why isn't the power of the Holy Ghost operating? You may possibly say, "I don't feel it." Is that because you are not willing to submit and surrender yourself unto the Holy Spirit in your heart, mind, soul, and body? It should not have anything to do with what is or is not going on in the church. The Bible reads, "O magnify the Lord with me, and let us exalt his name together" (Psalm 34:3 KJV).

We do not come to church to magnify humans. Rather, we come to the house of the Lord to magnify and glorify His name. In the church or in our daily lives, the Holy Ghost is right there with you, and you must first surrender unto Him. The power of the Holy Ghost shall reign over you if you just let Him. It is this authority and power of the Holy Ghost within you, and it is this authority and power of the Holy Ghost on high that ushers you into prayer, praise, and worship. God may use many other ways to get you to turn toward Him, but He will wait until the Holy Spirit has taken its proper place and position within you. Anything outside of that is a form of God.

We find ourselves acting and pretending based on what we have either seen or been taught. Tradition has bound you to humankind's ways of doing things, which have been passed down from generations ago. You find yourself acting almost like a puppet, waiting for someone to tell you what to do: stand up, sit down, pray, sing, clap your hands, stomp your feet, raise your hands, bring them down, say, "Amen," and say, "Hallelujah." You jump and shout because you enjoy the feeling of being entertained. But where is God? Where is the Holy Spirit? And where is Jesus Christ in the midst of all this entertainment?

I agree there must be some order within the church, but does it have to be so restrictive that God is not able to have complete freedom and control to move about? Instead, God is placed (that is, if He is even in it) on someone's timetable. If God is not being edified and glorified, then who is? Tradition has it that we are to act, perform, and present ourselves a certain way at various times during the service. There is no freedom to be truly free in the Spirit. Maybe this can explain why most Christians will not move, even if unctioned by the Holy Spirit. Maybe out of apprehension. Maybe the thought of other people looking at you and feeling a little shy and embarrassed. Or could it be the thought, *Since no one else is doing it, why should I? Then again, I could be chastised for acting out of order, and I should just control of myself.* I have visited many churches and places of fellowship with God and His people. I often felt so out of place because the service was being conducted like a game of "Simon says."

We are being bound by established traditions. In a way, humankind, not God, is the one really being edified and glorified. Yes, we must adhere to certain things. But must it be so time restrained (or restricted) that it feels like you are welcomed in, presented with just enough scripture or a message, asked to give an offering, told to come back next week, and ushered out so that you can do it all over again?

Instead of asking people how service was, I decided to ask people from different places, "What did God say or do in church today?" Their answers were pretty much the same. They would edify and glorify the music and the songs that were sung and the pastor or preacher who gave the message. But not once did anyone mention what God said or did. I thought, *Maybe they did not understand my question.* So I said, "What did God say to you?" Their responses really did not change. Well, the pastor, or the preacher said this or that. They still continued to edify everything but the name of the Lord. And at no time did the conversation ever include the Holy Ghost. I wondered if they even heard the voice of God while in the service. If it is of God, He will always speak to you through various ways—provided you are hearing from Him.

It is tradition that has caused a majority of Christians to focus on what is happening on the outside of them and then hoping it to be drawn on the inside with God. The truth of the matter is that from the outside-in is not how it works. Any attempt other than God's way is cut off and rejected. I have heard it said, "It must be caught, not just taught." Until you understand that God expresses Himself from the inside-out, you will never be able to experience a true relationship with God. You must first connect with God from within. He desires to express Himself out of you and then pull that which is of Him inside. This is the only way that you will be able to edify, glorify, magnify, and honor Him. Still, tradition wants God to recognize its works ahead of recognizing God's way.

Whether you want to believe it or not, most of God's people are "playing church." The Bible says, "And I say also unto thee, That thou art Peter, and upon this rock I will build my church; and the gates of hell shall not prevail against it" (Matthew 16:18 KJV). The kingdom of God is already here. God is letting it be known unto us that the time of playing church is over. Actually, it never began. But most institutions want to pretend like church is operating according to their ways. When you begin to allow the Holy Ghost to take full reign over your life, you begin to receive God's Word of truth. It is all about the kingdom of God, or it isn't about anything everlasting and eternal. Come to Him.

Denominational Doctrines. Words have meaning, and the meaning of those words can become one's reality. But reality isn't truth. Reality changes from one moment to the next. Yet truth never changes. Words can carry a power over us all on their own, whether they are spoken or written. The word "denomination" means a recognized, autonomous branch of the Christian church, religious group, sect, cult, movement, body, branch, persuasion, order, school, or church. A gathering of like-minded people.

The church is not only universal; it is local. It is not only corporate; it is individual. The church is the body of Christ (believers of Jesus Christ). The Bible reads,

> There is one body, and one Spirit, even as ye are called in one hope of your calling: one Lord, one faith, one baptism, one God and Father of all, who is above all, and through all, and in you all. (Ephesians 4:4–6 KJV)

With this in mind, why are there various denominations and doctrines that have created and caused division among the saints?

Which church or denomination should a person choose? Since all churches or denominations do not believe or practice the same way, choosing where to go can be like choosing which car to buy, deciding what foods to eat, deciding what clothing to wear, and so on. But how do you know when you did not know in the beginning? How can Jesus be found in every church or denomination since they teach and preach doctrines that are contradictory to each other's and God's Word? When you talk to people about their beliefs, they will try to defend their denominational doctrines as opposed to uplifting Jesus Christ, the Holy Ghost, or edifying God. This can make Jesus and the Bible appear ridiculous and hypocritical.

What can make the Bible seem ridiculous and hypocritical is how the Word of God is presented by the messengers from various denominations. God's Word of truth is being compromised by so many based on their doctrinal beliefs. Instead of preaching and teaching God's Word of truth, many speak only to motivate and entertain God's people. Some people simply say, "Oh, it does not really matter." That is an untruth! The Bible warns, "Whosoever transgresseth, and abideth not in the doctrine of Christ, hath not God. He that abideth in the doctrine of Christ, he hath both the Father and the Son" (2 John 9 KJV). In essence, it does matter whether God's Word of truth is presented, so the people of God can live out their lives according to His Word.

The Bible tells us,

> I Jesus have sent mine angel to testify [say] unto you these things in the churches. I am the root and the offspring of David, and the bright and morning star. And the Spirit and the bride say, Come. And let him that heareth say, Come. And let him that is athirst come. And whosoever will, let him take the water of life freely. For I testify [say] unto every man

that heareth the words of the prophecy [message] of this book, If any man shall add unto these things, God shall add unto him the plagues that are written in this book: and if any man shall take away from the words of the book of this prophecy [message], God shall take away his part out of the book of life [from the tree of life], and out of the holy city, and from the things which are written in this book. (Revelation 22:16–19 KJV)

What are you being feed? What are you feeding the people? Jesus told the apostle Peter to feed His lambs and sheep (John 21:15–18). After the Holy Ghost came, the apostle Paul was sent off on his evangelistic mission, and he told the elders at Ephesus to feed the church of God (Acts 20:22–29). The apostle Peter told strangers scattered throughout Pontus, Galatia, Cappadocia, Asia, and Bithynia to feed the flock (1 Peter 5:1–4). What were they to feed them: peanuts, popcorn, candy, and a soft drink? No. They were to be feed God's Word of truth. The apostle Paul says,

I [Apostle Paul] charge thee therefore before God, and the Lord Jesus Christ, who shall judge the quick [living] and the dead at his appearing and his kingdom; preach the word; be instant in season, out of season; reprove, rebuke, exhort [entreat] with all longsuffering and doctrine. For the time will come when they [God's people] will not endure [accept] sound doctrine, but after their own lusts shall they heap to themselves teachers, having itching ears; and they [God's people] shall turn away their ears from the truth, and shall be turned unto fables. But watch thou in all things, endure afflictions, do the work of an evangelist, make full proof of thy ministry. (2 Timothy 4:1–5 KJV)

When you begin to believe doctrines contrary to that of Jesus Christ, problems arise. Understand that truth does not contradict truth! Jesus taught and preached the uncompromised Word of God. Denominations, on the other hand, add to and take away from God's Word of truth to motivate and entertain their members. In fact, denominations contradict each other. How can it be that they are all teaching and preaching God's uncompromised Word of truth when there are contradictions?

God has a plan to save the souls of all His people into one universal body—the body of Christ. Yet, denominations still attempt to change God's plan knowingly or unknowingly by adding their own concept of doctrinal affiliation. Where in the Bible is there any spoken or written word about denominations? If there is nothing in the Bible, then denominations and their doctrines were established by humans and not God. The Bible tells us, "There is a way which seemeth right unto a man, but the end thereof are the ways of death" (Proverbs 14:12 KJV).

If we are really going to follow Jesus Christ without looking back and be attentive to God's ways and thoughts, we must pull down those strongholds of denominational doctrines in order to be obedient and without compromise only to God's Word of truth. Jesus said, "And ye shall know the truth, and the truth shall make you free" (John 8:32 KJV). God's truth does matter in our lives.

Imaginations. You are able to bring images out of your carnal mind and into your heart. There they can run rampant and free. These images, left unchecked, can either become your fancy or your reality. The Bible says,

> For though we walk in the flesh, we do not war after the flesh: (for the weapons of our warfare are not carnal, but mighty through God to the pulling down of strongholds;) casting down imaginations, and every high thing that exalteth itself against the

> knowledge of God, and bringing into captivity every thought to the obedience of Christ; and having in a readiness to revenge [avenge] all disobedience, when your obedience is fulfilled. (2 Corinthians 10:3–6 KJV)

We must be careful not to allow our minds to have dominion over us outside of the Holy Ghost.

If we are capable of thinking, wanting, or desiring something in our minds, we can make believe that it will or has come true. Then we can convince others people to support it. Today, the majority of Christians allow their imaginations is run free and operate according to their beliefs. This is a result of resisting the obedience and control of the Spirit of God. Our imaginations are those thoughts or fantasies about what you desire from this world system.

In our imaginations, we want and desire to do the things that we want to do, or to have the things we want to have. We have allowed things—stuff—to identify who we are and what we want to do. We have allowed our five senses—what we see, hear, feel, taste, and smell—to determine how we are to be, what things we want to do, and how we are going to go about it. To satisfy our desires, or false sense of needs, we will even mislead others. What becomes more important is that we are self-fulfilled above all others, including God. The Bible reads, "And God saw that the wickedness of man was great in the earth, and that every imagination of the thoughts of his heart was evil and continually [all the day]" (Genesis 6:5 KJV).

Some of our motives outside God's will include being completely disobedient and selfish. We may act and pretend like we are about one thing when we are actually doing something else for self-gratification. Your sins, pleasures, desires, needs, and greed have established their own places in your mind and heart. You are trying to walk them out with your hopes in your own achievements. Then there will be those who have decided to follow along. They are so happy just to be in the presence of it all. They have allowed someone else's imagination to become a part of their own lives.

But where is God? King David spoke to his son Solomon, saying, "And thou, Solomon, my son, know thou the God of thy father, and serve him with a perfect heart and with a willing mind: for the Lord searcheth all hearts, and understandeth all imaginations of the thoughts: if thou seek him, he will be found of thee; but if thou forsake him, he will cast thee off for ever" (1 Chronicles 28:9 KJV).

To pull down this stronghold of imagination, you must surrender and submit yourself to the Holy Ghost. The apostle Paul said,

> If there be therefore any consolation [comfort] in Christ, if any comfort of love, if any fellowship of the Spirit, if any bowels [affection] and mercies [compassion], fulfill ye my joy, that ye be likeminded, having the same love, being of one accord, of one mind. Let nothing be done through strife or vainglory; but in lowliness of mind let each esteem other better than themselves. Look not every man on his own things, but every man also on the things of others. Let this mind be in you, which was also in Christ Jesus: who, being in the form of God, thought it not robbery to be equal with God: but made himself of no reputation, and took upon him the form of a servant, and was made in the likeness of men: and being found in fashion as a man, he humbled himself, and became obedient unto death, even the death of the cross. (Philippines 2:1–8 KJV)

Pull down this stronghold of imagination. Become who God has predestined you to be, not what humanity or your imagination thinks or tries to get you to be. Then you will be able to do all that God has predestined for you.

Nations of Governmental Powers. Whatever nation or kingdom you have submitted yourself is the one you must yield to. The nations or kingdoms of this world have established their own individual powers and authority over all those who live within their borders. In the Bible, Jesus says, "I have given them thy word; and the world hath hated them, because they are not of this world, even as I am not of the world" (John 17:14 KJV). Nations or kingdoms desire that all you need to know and become is what they present to you and allow you to know.

God's Word of truth is in opposition to all nations or kingdoms. When you come into knowing God's Word of truth, you shall begin to turn from the wicked ways of that nation or kingdom and begin a journey of walking into the knowledge and understanding of God's Word of truth. The Bible says,

> Love not the world, neither the things that are in the world. If any man love the world, the love of the Father is not in him. For all that is in the world, the lust of the flesh, and the flesh of the eyes, and the pride of life, is not of the Father, but is of the world. And the world passeth away, and the lust thereof: but he that doeth [practices] the will of God abideth for ever. (1 John 2:15–17 KJV)

So who or what do you love? This question should not be taken for granted. Don't be so quick to answer. The answer must truthfully come from your heart and mind. It is only through God that you can come to the knowledge and understanding of this truth about love because love is God, and God is love. Satan has infiltrated our hearts and minds to the degree that "lust" wears the mask of love. It takes on the deception of fooling you into thinking it is love. You have accepted this lie as being love. Be honest, and call it for what it really is—lust. Stop acting and pretending that it is love. The truth is you do not know what love is, yet you do not want to call it lust.

But that is exactly what it is and what you are doing. You are lusting after stuff and each other for selfish reasons.

When Jesus was asked about paying tribute money (taxes), the Bible tells us,

> Shew me a penny [$32]. Whose image and superscription [inscription] hath it? They answered and said, Caesar's. And he said unto them, Render [give] therefore unto Caesar the things which be Caesar's, and unto [pay to] God the things which be God's. (Luke 20:24, 25 KJV)

It is all about your soul. If Satan and this world system—the nations of governmental powers—can create their wills over you, it will cause confusion and conflict within your heart and mind. Your soul will be held in captivity. Therefore, give what belongs to the world to the world; just don't become of or like the world.

Recognize that there is only one true kingdom. It is the kingdom of God, and it is there you will come to know how to walk and talk according to God's Word of truth. You will never be able to experience a right relationship with God until you forsake the ways of the world and receive the spirit of truth. The Bible reads,

> Let him that is taught in the word communicate [share with] unto him that teacheth in all good things. Be not deceived; God is not mocked: for whatsoever a man soweth, that shall he also reap. For he that soweth to his flesh shall of the flesh reap corruption [death]; but he that soweth to the Spirit shall of the Spirit reap life everlasting. (Galatians 6:6–8 KJV)

We must pull down this stronghold of nations of governmental powers so that it does not cause our hearts and minds to mirror the image of that nation or kingdom. We are under God. The Bible reads,

> I beseech you therefore, brethren, by the mercies of
> God, that ye present your bodies a living sacrifice,
> holy, acceptable unto God, which is your reasonable
> service. And be not conformed to this world: but be
> ye transformed by the renewing of your mind, that
> ye may prove what is that good, and acceptable, and
> perfect, will of God. (Romans 12:1, 2 KJV)

Theology of Humankind. I heard someone say, "Newer theology is not necessarily better theology." However, I believe that what is considered newer is just new, and what seems to be better is just better. When it comes to Christian theology, what is newer or better should come from the same source—the Spirit of God. It is God's revelation of His Word that is truth!

On December 27, 2015, Pastor Denise Folks of the Greater Church of the Risen Savior in Baltimore, Maryland, delivered an inspiring sermon titled "Tell the Truth; Know the Truth; Hear the Truth." This sermon touched me because I had completely hit a wall (or stalemate) in this portion of this book. As a matter of fact, everything else in the book had been completed except this one portion. As I sat there, hearing the words of God come through her spirit, I asked the Holy Ghost to intervene. It wasn't until she was at the very end of that message that the Holy Ghost said, "Write this down." Then He said, "When you have been given the ability to hear God's Word of truth, you will come to understand and know His Word of truth. Then, without compromise, you must speak of God's Word of truth. You may even have to repent for speaking what you might have misinterpreted as truth. However, now that you know, God will hold you accountable and responsible for speaking His uncompromised Word of truth." The Bible reads, "Jesus saith unto him [unto us], I am the way, the truth, and the life: no man cometh unto the Father, but by me" (John 14:6 KJV).

Any written or spoken message regarding Christian theology that does not speak on the uncompromised Word of truth and does not edify Christ is not of God. God's Word of truth is supposed to speak into the spirit, heart, mind, and soul from the perspective and revelation given by God through the Holy Ghost. Otherwise, theologians are using scriptures to express their own intellectual thoughts and opinions that enter the carnal mind of others.

Christian theologians rarely agree with each other because they are either using their own perspectives apart from God, they have completely misinterpreted scripture, or they attempt to esteem themselves as the authority for their theology that is in opposition to God. This creates and causes humankind's theology to be often misrepresentative of God's Word of truth and "warped."

Scripture is very essential, yet you can be given a higher revelation through the authority and power of the Spirit of God. When the Spirit of God, which is the Holy Ghost, speaks and tells you about this or that, you are not in the position to question or change what He has revealed unto you. It is the Spirit of God that revealed it, and it is the Spirit of God who will lead, guide, and provide you with God's Word of truth. You may not be able to explain it all properly or prove everything to someone else to get their approval. Let it be known that the Spirit of God is your witness, and by faith, you must not doubt. You are to stand firm on God's Word of truth, and at His appointed time, He shall reveal that which has been written or spoken.

The theology of humankind has changed quite a bit over the years. It has become more about what the theologian has said to be the truth than what God says is truth. In many cases, they even question what has been stated by God. With so many theologies, there is a lack of agreement among them, and that brings confusion and division. So who's right, and who's wrong? Christian theologians must first look to God for their expressions of God and the scriptures.

Theology can bring about a watered-down expression of God's Word to accentuate their own thoughts and opinions.

When theologians convey their messages, they come primarily from a reality of their present time of thoughts. As I have said earlier in this book, there is a reality of life that we live in, but it changes from one moment to the next. Reality, as real as it may be, is not the truth! Truth never changes; it is constant. Yet it grows from with added revelations by God. For with Christ it all does matter!

Chapter 7

Which Way Is Up?

I am the way, the truth, and the life: no man cometh unto the Father, but by me.

John 14:6 KJV

ONE OF THE MANY QUESTIONS that we must ask ourselves is, Where am I going? We must come to know this for ourselves. There is a destiny we must keep even though there will be various destinations (or reference points) along the way. This is not a question or an answer that you should take lightly. It cannot be just some simple repeated response based on what you have heard others say. How will you know? Even more so, how will others know, or are they only repeating what they have heard? This question can only be answered through the guidance of the Holy Ghost. It may not be fully revealed, but the Holy Ghost shall lead you in the right direction with God's instructions about you are to go and what you are to do. Your submission and surrender to the Holy Ghost will take away any doubts or fears. It will be those things that are revealed by the Holy Ghost which you must live out in your life.

When asked if they are going to heaven, many people just simply say, "Yes, I am going to heaven." But when pressed further, very few can say with certainty that they are going to heaven. Or they may simply keep repeating what they have heard others say, or try to quote something from scripture. This is all good, but the question that would still leave many others puzzled is, "Did the Lord thy God tell you so?"

Until the Lamb's Book of God is opened, you will not know for sure. So what are you going to do now to prepare yourself for that time? Could it be that the reason the vast majority of people are unable to truthfully answer these questions is because they have not surrendered and submitted themselves to the Holy Ghost? When you hear people professing their relationship with God and Jesus Christ, they say little to nothing regarding the essence of the Holy Ghost. It is the Holy Ghost who will guide, instruct, protect, and comfort you in all things of God and who edifies Jesus Christ. There can be no true relationship with Jesus Christ without the Holy Ghost. For it is the Holy Ghost that leads us to Jesus Christ, and it is Jesus Christ that leads us to the Father. Therefore, without the Holy Ghost, your relationship with God is in vain. Your destiny begins and ends with God through His Spirit—the Holy Ghost. When you start developing your relationship with the Holy Ghost, you are also establishing your relationship with Jesus Christ and God the Father. It is God who gives us the provision, authority, power, and protection through the Holy Ghost. By His Spirit, our heart, mind, and soul are open to His Word, His thoughts, and His ways for our lives' destiny. The Bible says,

> Trust in the Lord with all thine heart, and lean not unto thine own understanding. In all thy ways acknowledge him, and he shall direct thy paths. (Proverbs 3:5, 6 KJV)

The Holy Ghost is essential!

As discussed previously, there are some who claim there are other roads leading to the kingdom of God. This is not true. There are some who know the truth, but they will not speak against or correct those who have spoken outside the Word of God. According to Jesus, "I am the way, the truth, and the life: no man cometh unto the Father, but by me" (John 14:6 KJV). The Bible says,

> Enter ye in at the strait gate: for wide is the gate, and broad is the way, that leadeth to destruction, and many there be which go in thereat: because strait is the gate, and narrow is the way, which leadeth unto life, and few there be that find it. (Matthew 7:13, 14 KJV)

Without the guidance of the Holy Ghost, you are lost. The only way to Jesus Christ is by the Holy Ghost, and the only way to the kingdom of God is by Jesus Christ. So the only way to the Father is also through Jesus Christ.

Picture, if you will, an entryway (the strait gate). There are so many broad ways to travel. Yet it is only the one, narrow way of Jesus Christ that leads you to the Father and into the kingdom of God. Without the Holy Ghost, who knows the way, you would be traveling in a direction where you will end up wandering around or coming to a dead end, like being in a maze. Because you decide not to follow the Holy Ghost, you will find yourself walking through this maze of life called the world system. Get right with God through the Holy Ghost. Repent, pray, seek God, ask for forgiveness, submit and surrender, walk in obedience, have faith, and trust God. God shall, according to His grace and mercy, forgive you and provide a way out of nowhere to Himself. God will open a door that you did not see so that you will be able to reconnect with His Spirit. Why? Because the Bible tells us,

> For God so loved the world, that he gave his only begotten Son, that whosoever believeth in him should not perish, but have everlasting life. For God sent not his Son into the world to condemn the

world; but that the world through him might be saved. He that believeth on Him is not condemned: but he that believeth is condemned already, because he hath not believeth in the name of the only begotten Son of God. And this is the condemnation [judgment], that light is come into the world, and men loved darkness rather than light, because their deeds were evil. For everyone that doth evil hateth the light, neither cometh to the light, lest his deeds should be reproved [examined]. But he that doeth truth cometh to the light, that his deeds may be made manifest, that they are wrought [shaped] in God. (John 3:16–21 KJV)

We must understand that the only way to heaven is through the shed blood and resurrection of Jesus Christ. Still, there are those who believe there is another way, and they mislead others according to their own beliefs and doctrines.

The Roman Catholic Church, by the authority of the pope at that time, instituted its own beliefs and doctrines regarding the idea of purgatory. It has been believed that Pope Gregory the Great, who reigned from A.D. 590 – 604, invented the doctrine of purgatory to make money. This belief has also influenced many other denominations. According to the Roman Catholic doctrine, there is an intermediate state or place after physical death. It is a place of suffering for the souls of sinners who are in the process of removing their sin and guilt. In this place, these souls undergo purification to become holy enough to enter heaven.

By misinterpreting and misunderstanding of 1 Corinthians 3:15, they hold to the evidence of purgatory. The Bible reads, "If any man's work shall be burned, he shall suffer loss: but he himself shall be saved: yet so as by fire." What they failed to include were a few earlier verses. This particular portion of scripture allowed them to lean to their own understanding for their own purposes.

The apostle Paul said to the church at Corinth,

> According to the grace of God which is given unto me, as a wise masterbuilder, I have laid the foundation, and another buildeth thereon. But let every man take heed how he buildeth thereon. For other foundation can no man lay than is laid, which is Jesus Christ. Now if any man build upon this foundation gold, silver, precious stones, wood, hay, stubble; every man's work shall be made manifest: for the day shall declare it, because it shall try every man's work of what sort it is. If any man's work abide which he hath built thereupon, he shall receive a reward. If any man's work shall be burned, he shall suffer loss: but he himself shall be saved; yet so as [through] the fire. (1 Corinthians 3:10–15 KJV)

The Roman Catholic Church purposely did this to downplay Jesus Christ's suffering, sacrifice, and authority.

To begin with, this portion of scripture speaks of the foundation of all things that were in Jesus Christ. Any other foundation being set was not of Jesus Christ but of whoever tried to lay it. Second, God would eventually judge the works of the believers through the fire. If their works were good, it would not be consumed by the fire, and they would receive a reward. But if their works were unsatisfactory, it would be consumed by the fire, and they would not receive a reward. And third, believers did not go through fire; only their works did. We must not look at things as they appear to be, but look beyond to what they are. In other words, it may seem that one's works prosper here on earth, but when God judges that work in the fire, it may have been of the world and not of God.

The Catholic Church established its own foundation by the authority of the pope. It indicated that Jesus Christ's sacrifice was insufficient and incomplete. They believed that one's works was equal to and connected to one's salvation. However, the apostle Paul said,

> Moreover, brethren, I declare unto you the gospel which I preached unto you, which also ye have received, and wherein ye stand; by which also ye are saved, if ye keep in memory what I preached unto you, unless ye have believed in vain [without cause]. For I delivered unto you first of all that which I also received, how that Christ died for our sins according to the scriptures; and that he was buried, and that he rose again the third day according to the scriptures. (1 Corinthians 15:1–4 KJV)

Search the scriptures for "purgatory." The teachings of purgatory, according to the doctrine of the Catholic Church, contradicts all the teachings of Jesus Christ, the understanding of who God is, and His sacrifice. This includes what the apostle Paul reaffirmed regarding Jesus Christ. According to the Catholic Church, purgatory offers a second opportunity, apart from Jesus Christ, to be saved. In truth, purgatory is neither scriptural nor biblical.

With this being said about purgatory, why is it still reinforced in churches today? Do not be puzzled or confused. When you research this, you will discover that purgatory is actually a business established and instituted by the Catholic Church by the authority of Pope Benedict XVI. He announced that it would return, and those seeking a way into heaven can pay their way for it through the church. In the February 10, 2009, *New York Times,* it is reported that even though the church officially broke with its old practice of "You do something good for me, and the church will help do something good for you," in 1960, Pope John XXIII quietly reintroduced it back into the church. The Catholic Church was banned from the practice of selling indulgences in 1567. Anyway, the *New York Times* pointed out that a monetary donation wouldn't go amiss toward earning an indulgence. It reported, "Charitable contributes combined with other acts, can help you earn one." You can even buy indulgences this way for loved ones who are already dead, easing their way to heaven by doing something for the church here on earth.

Why would the Catholic Church agree to this reversal? Did it have anything to do with the economy or the church's fading influences? A bishop from Brooklyn, New York, told the reporter, "Not at all, because there is sin in the world."

Likewise, there are others in various denominations that simply use Jesus Christ as a means to make money. You have a decision to make. You can either continue to stay where you are (mind-set), and go along with what you have been taught and told (settling for the ways of the world church system), or you can go out on your own (repent) with the hope of finding the way to Jesus Christ through the Holy Ghost and demand to be told of God's Word of truth. It is the Holy Ghost that will bring forth the knowledge and understanding in knowing that the only way to heaven is through the shed blood and resurrection of Jesus Christ. It is the Holy Ghost that will reveal God's Word of truth. God shall direct your path of purpose and destiny.

There will still be some who continue in a doctrine that is not according to God's uncompromised truth. The Bible says,

> Now therefore fear the Lord, and serve him in sincerity and in truth: and put away the gods which your fathers served on the other side of the flood, and in Egypt; and serve ye the Lord. And if it seem evil unto you to serve the Lord, choose you this day whom ye will serve; whether the gods which your fathers served that were on the other side of the flood, or the gods of the Amorites, in whose land ye dwell: but as for me and my house, we will serve the Lord. (Joshua 24:14, 15 KJV)

For with Christ it all does matter!

CONCLUSION

GOD HAS PROVIDED US WITH His Word of truth. God has given us His only begotten Son. And God has sent us His Spirit, the Holy Ghost. The Bible tells us,

> Let this mind be in you, which was also in Christ Jesus: who, being in the form of God, thought it not robbery to be equal with God: but made himself of no reputation, and took upon him the form of a servant, and was made in the likeness of men: and being found in fashion as a man, he humbled himself, and became obedient unto death, even the death of the cross. (Philippians 2:5–8 KJV)

God's Word of truth is continuously being revealed, so we may enter the kingdom of God. However, there is a large majority of God's people who stand just outside the kingdom. They failed to realize that the kingdom of God is just on the other side. If only they knew, they would be able to walk in His truth.

It is your personal responsibility to hear His Word, see His Word, read His Word, and then follow His Word to live out your life according to His plan and purpose. The choice is yours as to whether you will receive and accept God's uncompromised Word of truth for your life or continue to receive and accept a truth from humankind that may have been compromised.

What has been presented in this book are just a few truths about God's Word that you must come to know. There will be two other books forthcoming. The Bible reads, "For my thoughts are not your thoughts, neither are your ways my ways, saith the Lord" (Isaiah 55:8 KJV). As true as this is, God can reveal His thoughts and His ways through the Holy Ghost as He so chooses. We must begin to totally submit and surrender ourselves to God, be obedient unto His Law and commands, have the faith to believe that God is who He says He is, and then come to know God's Word of truth. We can then rightly speak His Word of truth. Then, and only then, will you be able to speak the same words as Joshua: "But as for me and my house, we will serve the Lord" (Joshua 24:15). Let the Holy Ghost direct, instruct, and guide you in all the things of God. Because with Christ it all does matter!

Contact Information:

God's Word of Truth Ministries, LLC

P.O. Box 66217

Baltimore, MD 21239-9998

Printed in the United States
By Bookmasters